How do we eradicate the ro
build a culture of atonemen

This rare, insightful book discusses the great moral issues of
sin and redemption against the collective backdrop of the
terrorist attacks on New York, the Enron debacle, and the
Pedophilia scandal of the Catholic Church. It is certain to
become required reading in divinity schools, law schools, and
criminal justice programs across the country!

Paul Ferrini's books are the most important I have read.
I study them like a Bible.

ELISABETH KÜBLER-ROSS

Paul Ferrini's writing will inspire you to greater insights
and understandings, to more clarity and a grander resolve
to make changes in your life that can truly change the world.

NEALE DONALD WALSCH

Paul Ferrini is an important teacher in the new millennium.
Reading his work has been a major awakening for me.

IYANLA VANZANT

Paul Ferrini is a modern day Kahlil Gibran— poet, mystic,
visionary, teller of truth.

LARRY DOSSEY

Paul Ferrini reconnects us to the Spirit Within,
to that place where even our deepest wounds can be healed.

JOAN BORYSENKO

Book Design by Paul Ferrini
and Lisa Carta

Cover Art: *The Fall* by Raphael
Pg. 12 and 56: *Eve* by Albrecht Dürer
Pg. 102: *The Fall* by Hugo van der Goes
Pg. 114: *The Allegory of Earth* by Jan Brueghel the Elder

ISBN 1-879159-48-1

Library of Congress Control Number: 20022106490

Manufactured in the United States of America

Heartways Press
P.O. Box 99, Greenfield MA 01302

Manufactured in the United States of America

FORBIDDEN FRUIT

Unraveling the Mysteries of Sin, Guilt and Atonement

PAUL FERRINI

TABLE OF CONTENTS

Introduction 7

1   The Fall 13

2   Wings 23

3   Imperfection 33

4   Correction or Punishment? 43

5   Light in the Dark Places 57

6   Terror & Collective Guilt 69

7   Moving out of Denial 85

8   Mapping the Territory 103

9   Opening the Garden Gate 115

INTRODUCTION

When I was a child, I loved the Uncle Remus stories. One of my favorite stories was about Brer Rabbit, Brer Fox and the Tar Baby.

Brer Fox decided to pay Brer Rabbit back for some troubles in the past so he created a baby made of tar. Brer Rabbit walked right into the trap. He tried handle the Tar-Baby and got stuck.

Brer Fox laughed heartily as he watched Brer Rabbit try in vain to disentangle himself, and he threatened to do all kinds of terrible things to his captive. However, Brer Rabbit was smarter than Brer Fox realized. To every threat Brer Fox made, Brer Rabbit responded "I don't care what you do with me so long as you don't fling me in that briar patch."

Of course, Brer Fox wanted to put the most hurt on Brer Rabbit, so he decided to throw him in the briar patch. Brer Rabbit got exactly what he wanted by using "reverse psychology."

Even though the briar patch wasn't exactly a comfortable place, it helped Brer Rabbit scrape off some of the tar from his fur and he eventually was able to regain his freedom.

Now my hunch is that God was at least as smart as Brer Rabbit. And He too was not adverse to using a little "reverse psychology." When He pointed out the Tree of Knowledge in the Garden of Eden and told Adam and Eve not to eat its fruits, He knew that the first thing they would want to do was go and taste that forbidden fruit.

Adam and Eve were not just naughty, disobedient children.

They were created in God's image. They had God's desire for creative expression and awareness. As long as they remained in the Garden, they could not take the next step in their evolution.

God was a bit of a trickster. He knew that Adam and Eve would not leave the safety of the Garden unless they were made an offer that they could not refuse. So God sent the Serpent to them to make the offer.

The Serpent didn't have to twist any arms. He simply found a way to give Adam and Eve permission to do what they really wanted to do. He helped them overcome their fears and take a risk.

That's what the creative principle requires of us. We must leave behind what is familiar and safe and take the risk of exploring the unknown. That's the bold choice Adam and Eve made.

Each one of us is offered the same choice at certain crucial points in our lives. The story is numinous and allegorical, after all. It conveys something that is true about all of us.

No, it was not divine error that placed the Tree of Knowledge or the Serpent in the Garden. It was divine intuition. How do you convince a dependent, obedient child to leave home, especially if there is a comfortable bed and three gourmet meals served every day? Adam and Eve weren't going to make a conscious choice to leave the comforts of the Garden.

The choice had to be made at an unconscious level. They were driven by a desire that they did not yet understand.

Of course, all that came afterward would be about understanding the choice they had made. Once they ate the forbidden fruit, Adam and Eve began a spiritual journey that would take them from sin to atonement, from ignorance to knowledge, from denial to responsibility.

Although learning the difference between good and evil would be a very confusing affair for Adam and Eve and their descendants, it would eventually help them to reclaim the innocence and perfection they seemed to have left behind in their journey to conscious creation.

As the world turns once again to deal with the perpetrators of mass murder, some of us may kneel humbly before the altar and wonder if God let us have a little too much freedom. It is not the first time human beings have wondered if the choice we made to leave the safety of the Garden was the right one.

Even Moses had a moment of dread on his way down from Mt. Sinai with the tablets of the law. He knew that human beings had a knack of making things mean what they wanted them to mean. "What would happen if 'thou shalt not kill' should be interpreted 'thou shalt not kill people who believe in your God?'"

Being close to God, Moses could not help but understand the concept of the briar patch. Tell people not to do something and they will line up at the gate.

Commandments are good for people who are obedient to authority, but every society has its share of troublemakers. And they have to find things out for themselves. That's just the way it is.

Serpent energy is our desire for experience. It is the

energy of incarnation. It is the reason we want to be here. We want to learn to understand and master the world around us. And we also want to understand who we are. Our quest for knowledge takes us away from the certainties of the divine into the uncertainties of human experience. It takes us into a world where love is conditional and money, sex, name and fame become substitutes for the genuine love and acceptance we all want. Only when we realize that these substitutes do not satisfy do most of us begin a quest for a deeper meaning.

In the end, we discover that we came into this world for a simple reason. It wasn't to get rich or to get married and have babies, even though we can learn from all these things.

We came into this world to learn to love without conditions, to learn to create in a caring and responsible manner. And everything that happens to us here conspires toward this end.

The myth of the fall tells us that we were expelled from the Garden and are therefore worthy of God's wrath, but this is not true. The truth is that we came here with God's blessing. His spiritual laws followed us into this world of conditions and it is up to us to find them and embrace them.

Had we not eaten of the forbidden fruit from the Tree of the Knowledge of Good and Evil, we would not have left the Garden. We would not have become creative beings nor would we have learned to take responsibility for our creations. In eating the forbidden fruit, we were given the opportunity to make mistakes and learn from them, to become more aware and responsible for our actions.

We became sinners not to be shamed and punished indefinitely, but to discover the blueprint for our own redemption. In this way, we could realize God's vision for us when he created us in His image.

I

THE FALL

We left the garden of our innocence
not because we were forced to,
but because we wanted to learn to create.
We were not satisfied being "the created" children of God.
We did not want to be the work of art,
but to be artist him or herself.

The myth of the fall from grace is telling but inaccurate. We were not punished by God for leaving the Garden. We simply took a risk. We left behind our safe, secure and predictable life where love was given to us without conditions for a life in which we would have to learn to love and take care of ourselves.

In the Garden, we were eternal children. We simply did as we were told and all of our needs were met. We did not have to be creative, nor did we have to learn to take responsibility for our creations.

But we wanted to do this. We wanted to learn to create and to be responsible. That was the reason why we ate the forbidden fruit from the Tree of Knowledge. It was not the trickery of the Serpent that tempted us against our wills. No, we were ready to bite into the apple.

If God did not bless our journey of creation, He would not have put that tree in the Garden. Of course, he knew that knowledge was a double edged sword. He knew that what we learned might hurt us as well as help us.

He knew that leaving the Garden would open the doors of both heaven and hell. He knew that. That is why He warned us about the tree and its fruit.

Knowledge has a price. We decided that we were willing to pay that price.

I'm sure that there are many times every day when God looks at us and thinks we bit off a lot more than we could chew. Life on the other side of the wall of bliss is not easy. Yet, in spite of the hardship, there are not many of us who would be willing to go back. Bitch and moan as we may, most of us want to learn the lessons that arose with our freedom.

Indeed, even those who join cults looking for some salvation on high—be it from a spaceship or from an archangel—are forced to come back to earth sooner or later. Once you have chosen freedom, you cannot give it up. It's one of those defining moments.

That doesn't mean that people don't try. There are people in every religion selling admission tickets back to the Garden. Unfortunately, the only garden they are going to find is the one that Jesus stayed in before he was crucified.

The world of human beings is not a very nice place. People may want to learn how to be responsible for their actions, but for most of us it's a long learning curve.

DO UNTO OTHERS

When Jesus of Nazareth came on the scene, he understood the depth of the challenge that we were facing, but he was a tough teacher. He would not stand for any kind of pretense or self-deception. He demanded complete honesty.

If you hung out with Jesus, you couldn't pretend to love God or to love other people. You had to demonstrate your love or acknowledge your fear. There was no other choice.

You could fool a lot of people, but you could not fool Jesus. He knew your heart, even if you didn't.

His teaching was not particularly complicated or esoteric. He simply asked us to treat others as we would like to be treated. He asked us to be equals, to forgive each other's trespasses, to remember that we are here to learn how to love everyone, including our enemies.

He reminded us that although we left the Garden, we were not cut off from God's love. Indeed, he told us that only the love of God could sustain us through the many challenges we would face in our journey of conscious awakening.

Of course, the first thing people wanted to do was to make Jesus special. Some people thought Jesus had some special relationship with God. Others thought he was dangerous because people listened to him, so they convinced themselves that "Jesus was the problem."

Actually, Jesus was neither the problem nor the solution. He was simply someone who was not afraid to tell the truth. And even though he too inherited this post-Garden experience, he still remembered God's love for him.

He never believed even for a moment that God was punishing him or anyone else for wanting to know. Quite the contrary. He knew that leaving the Garden was in divine order.

The great tragedy of the decision to leave was not the loss of God's love, but the loss of the memory of God's love. The first thing Adam and Eve did when they left the Garden was to cover their private parts. They were ashamed of their creative potential. They believed that they were bad for leaving and that God was angry at them.

SHAME

Our problem then and now is the same one, notwithstanding the efforts of Jesus and the other great prophets to change our minds. We still feel that God is angry at us. We still feel that we are unworthy of His love.

When we left the Garden and had to make our first independent decision, we were absolutely terrified. "What happens if we make a mistake? What happens if we make the wrong choice?"

In the Garden, we just followed the rules, so we couldn't make a wrong choice. Someone else was calling the shots. Someone else had ultimate responsibility for what transpired.

But now, outside the gates, we trembled with fear. If we made a mistake, "God would punish us," or so we thought.

But this was just an illusion that arose from our separation anxiety. Once we ate from the Tree of Knowledge, the responsibility for our choices and their consequences was given to us. If anyone was going to punish us, it was not going to be God.

God was off the hook, and we were on it. That was a fait au complete.

OUR MISTAKES DO NOT CONDEMN US

So the first lesson we had to learn when we left paradise was a simple one: our mistakes do not condemn us. We were going to make mistakes whether we wanted to or not. There was nothing to be done about it. Making mistakes was part of the process of learning about our creative power. We had to master the functioning of our bodies and our minds. Like a toddler learning to walk, we were going to keep falling down until we learned to find our balance. It was a slow, tedious process, but a necessary one.

Sure, it was natural to be looking over our shoulders every time that we fell down, just to see if God was mad at us. But we had to learn to stop looking back. We had to learn to look ahead, to trust in our process.

That meant that we had to accept our mistakes and learn from them. It seems like a small matter, yet for us it was a huge paradigm shift. We had gone from being perfect and mistake free to being imperfect and mistake prone. It was easy to judge ourselves as being unworthy. It was easy to shame ourselves and our brothers and sisters.

17

The idea that we could make a mistake and still be love-able was a new concept for us. Moreover, the idea that we could learn from our mistakes and become more skillful and confident to boot seemed a strange one. Some of us pretended to understand when we didn't really. Either we did not understand the rules of the new game or we did not buy them.

The paradigm shifted, to be sure, but not all of us shifted with it. Some of us were still pulling a heavy sled behind us through the snow. It was an invisible sled, but that didn't make it any lighter. No matter what we accomplished, we kept turning around to see if there was a smile or a frown on God's face.

"Were we acceptable? Did we do good?" we couldn't help asking. We were walking around in adult bodies, but we still felt like children. We wanted mommy's and daddy's approval.

It didn't matter that mommy and daddy were not around any more. We carried them with us. Their shadows loomed heavily over our empty sleds as we trudged through the snow.

God had left us on our own, but that didn't stop us from looking for Him and personifying Him. It is not surprising that in the first phase of our post-Garden experience, we personified God as Mommy or Daddy. Some of us still do, even though there have been several shifts in the paradigm since then. So here we are, still asking "Did I do it right? Am I okay, God? Do you still love me?"

Let's not worry about how infantile this sounds. Let's be

honest so that we can see where we really stand.

So now every time we make a mistake—even though we all profess to know the rules of the game—we take a deep breath and wait for the thunderbolt to drop. You see, we say we get it, but we really don't. We really don't buy this idea that we are "free" to make mistakes.

THE PRICE OF FREEDOM

Free to make mistakes, free to fail, free to sin, to miss the mark, to err: what does this mean? What is this free will business, anyway?

Well, it is developmental, you could say. First your parents protect you and keep you safe, and then you have to learn to do this for yourself. Every bird needs to leave the nest sooner or later, no matter how great his fear of flying. Parents push you out the door when you take up too much room in the nest. "Build your own nest," they tell you.

You see, it is a law of the natural world. Small critters grow up to be big critters and big critters have to learn to fend for themselves.

So what does all this have to do with God, you ask?

Well, in eternity, there is no growing up: no birth, no death, no mistakes, no learning, no transformation. There is just unmitigated goodness. You don't feel separate from God. You don't feel separate from anyone else.

There is only one thing missing: you don't know who you are! You are not unique, individual, special. You are part of the whole, but you don't know what part you are.

That's the mystery of God. You play whatever part needs to be played. There is no ego, no competition for roles, no striving. You do what needs to be done: end of story.

"What about me God?" you asked. And of course, that was the beginning of the end. Did you think that God would not acknowledge you, even though he knew you were asking for trouble?

Of course not.

"Are you sure you want to know?" He replied.

"Yes, I think so," you said. You were just curious. You had no idea what you were getting into.

But God just laughed and told you "It will be okay." You see He knew that it was natural for you to want to know yourself. He knew that your desire to know and to experience could never be turned away. So He just pointed to the tree and said. "There you go. Find out for yourself."

You gave up bliss and absolute safety to know the truth. You entered the world of conditions naively but with a strange confidence. And that is because part of God went with you.

When the great paradigm shift happened, you could no longer find God outside you. You looked all over for Him, but He could not be found. Yet you felt His presence. Indeed, you kept hearing a little voice that said: "Here I am. I'm right here."

You see, that limitless light of divinity that seemed to disappear when the shift occurred went somewhere. Indeed that spark of the divine went right into your heart.

How else can you explain this inner knowing, this confidence, this clarity and this grace which appears when you listen deeply enough? In those times, you know that God is with you.

But there are other times when you forget about this indwelling spark. You feel alone in the world. You feel tired and beaten down and you don't know how you can go on. You are sure that God—if He exists at all—must hate you.

You disconnect from your own center, and then the world around you seems to come crashing down. You forget the freedom you asked for. You forget that you were the one who pleaded to be allowed entrance to this world of conditions.

You wanted to know who you are, and so you entered a world in which everyone tried to remake you in their own image. Understanding who you are and being it was a lot more difficult than you thought it would be. This was a world in which people pretended to know when they didn't know. It was a world of masks and shadows, a world where people hurt each other inadvertently, and not so inadvertently!

The world of human conditions did not satisfy. It did not feel safe. And so you began to wonder if you had made the right choice.

Was knowledge worth the price of your safety? And even if it was, did you really learn anything at all?

Here you were feeling separate from yourself and from your brother and sister, feeling miserable, broken and not up to the task you had taken on when you hear that little voice in your heart say "Don't worry. It will be okay. Just get up and try again."

"Just get up and try again? You must be kidding!"

"No, I'm not kidding. Get up now and be a little more gentle with yourself. Just do the best you can and you'll see. Everything will be all right."

"Are you sure?"

"Yes. I am sure, because I remember why you made this choice and I know that you cannot fail."

GET UP OR STAY ON THE GROUND?

So now comes the second choice. Do you get up or stay on the ground? Do you remember that you made the choice and begin to be responsible for it, or do you blame someone else and pretend to be a victim?

If you choose to be a victim, you will experience hell on earth. You will make mistakes and blame others instead of facing your mistakes and learning from them. And others, in turn, will blame you for the lessons they are afraid to learn. Your world will be a world of mutual fear, trespass, and retribution. It will be a human hell, from which you can escape only by taking responsibility.

Presumably, one day the pain of living such a life will be more than you can bear. And then you will be asked the question again: "Will you get up or stay on the ground? Do you choose to remain a victim or to take responsibility for what you have created?"

The gates of hell open or close depending on how you answer this question. You hold the key to the prison door. Whether you use it or not is up to you.

2

WINGS

Did we fall or jump from the citadel of grace?
Those who say we fell are simply not aware of the paradigm shift.
The truth is that the appendages sprouting on the sides of our backs
felt awkward and ungainly. We needed space to accommodate them.
And when the wind blew, we felt a stirring in our blood
we had not felt before.

Yes, the myth of the fall has certain inaccuracies. For one thing, it doesn't make any reference to the wings we were growing.

It doesn't tell us how life in the Garden had become predictable and boring. It doesn't talk about our need to grow and be challenged. It doesn't mention our need to individuate. It just says that we disobeyed God and were cast out of the Garden.

The truth is that we had to leave the Garden. We had no choice. We had to become conscious. We had to learn. We had to grow.

In this sense, sin was inevitable. Indeed, the very first sin was our desire to know. It set in motion a chain of events which continues to unfold.

Now sin may be inevitable. But it is not necessarily evil or bad. If our mistakes serve some higher purpose such as growth and transformation, then they can't be bad. They are simply part of a process.

Nobody enjoys being wrong. No one wants to make a fool out of herself. It is not pleasant to be caught with your hand in the cookie jar.

But, if it happens to all of us, then what's all the fuss?

Why do most of us believe that we are bad, evil or unworthy if we make a mistake? What is this shame all about?

Perhaps it has something to do with our guilt at leaving the Garden. As soon as Adam and Eve left the Garden, they felt shame. They covered their sexual organs—the symbol of their creative power. They wanted to hide their power.

Why is that?

Because they assumed that if they could create independently of God they would lose God's love and acceptance. In the past, they simply did God's Will, so mistakes were impossible and God's love was guaranteed. Now, for the first time, they had the power to create on their own. So what would happen if they created something God did not want? What if their will opposed His Will?

They assumed that God would be unhappy with them and he would withdraw his love from them. Perhaps they even believed that God would punish them for their mistakes. So anticipating the withdrawal of God's love or His retribution, as the case may be, the first humans were uncomfortable with their capacity to create on their own.

Their shame was a kind of anticipation of their ultimate guilt. Sooner or later, they would create something that would make God angry and they would lose his love and support.

Imagine the difficulty you would have exercising your creativity if you thought that by so doing you were going to lose love and support and you will see the dilemma Adam and Eve and the rest of us inherited.

As soon as you have free will, you have to come to terms with the potential for error. That's why Adam and Eve had two children: Cain and Able. Cain represented the capacity for error and Able the capacity for good.

EMBRACING CAIN

Of course we would all like to have Able without having his brother. But that would be impossible. Unless there is the potential for error, free will means nothing. If we can choose only good and not evil, only Able and not Cain, then we are not choosing at all. That lack of choice was a condition of the Garden. This potential to choose—with all its poignancy—is a condition of life outside the Garden walls.

Here, sin is a reality. People will make mistakes. Cain will take Able's life because he is jealous of him. There will be errors, both small and large; some understandable, some beyond anyone's comprehension.

And we will have to learn from our mistakes. We will have to find a way to atone for our transgressions.

When Moses came down from Mt. Sinai with the tablets of the law, it all seemed very simple. Here were ten simple actions that were either encouraged or forbidden. Simply perform certain actions and refrain from others and you could stay aligned with the Divine Will. The Ten Commandments were a kind of insurance policy against the trials and tribulations of post-Garden life.

Unfortunately, these commandments were a great deal more ambitious than they appeared to be. Adhering to these commandments was like saying to someone "Don't look at that yellow spot on the wall." 75% of the people you say that to are going to look at the yellow spot.

No matter how good an insurance policy you have—and no doubt every religion thinks it has the best one—people are going to continue to make choices that bring suffering to themselves and others. The question is not "Will the law be broken?" We already know the answer to that question. The question is "When the law is broken, how do you atone and make amends for the suffering you have caused?"

GUILT AND ATONEMENT

In order to atone, you must first know that you have made a mistake. Usually you know that you have made a mistake because you feel bad about your action. You see that it has caused suffering for yourself or for another. Perhaps you wish you could take that action back and make another choice. Perhaps you feel moved to apologize to others for the difficulty you caused them. Your guilt is simply the recognition of your mistake.

Atonement is a way of taking responsibility for the pain

and suffering caused by your errors. Just as you would accept the acknowledgement of others for actions you took that benefited them you also accept the testimony and criticism of those who have been hurt by your actions.

The goal of Atonement is a simple one. It is to correct, to take what has gone astray and bring it back into alignment. While sin is a missing of the mark, atonement is a reconnection with mark. When we sin, we get sidetracked; we cannot achieve an outcome that is good for us and for others. When we atone, we consciously move toward such a mutually beneficial outcome.

Sin often happens unconsciously. We make a mistake because we are not paying attention. Or it happens through our ignorance. We act on assumptions that simply aren't true.

Atonement is a correction of those false assumptions. It is a movement to pay attention in a way that we never have before.

Of course, the greatest false assumption is that we can benefit ourselves by hurting or taking advantage of others. That assumption may have been so reinforced in our lives that it is very difficult to correct.

To correct a false assumption you must first see that it is false. You cannot atone for a mistake if you don't think that you made one.

Understanding our error is essential if we are to move from sin to atonement. And guilt is the psychological mechanism that allows us to do this.

However, to experience our guilt, we cannot project it. As long as we are denying our feelings of discomfort or regret, as long as we are blaming, shaming or attacking someone else, we cannot look at our own thoughts and actions with any kind of honesty.

To experience our guilt, we have to come to terms with all of our thoughts and feelings and we need to see and feel the effects our actions have on others.

If we don't do this, we repress our guilt. It becomes hidden or unconscious. And then our guilt drives us without our being aware of it.

FACING OUR GUILT

So here's the rub. Who wants to sit with feelings of discomfort? Who wants to feel his pain and the pain of others? Who wants to uncover his own ignorance and false assumptions? This is not pleasant work.

It's much easier to play the game of denial and projection. It's much easier to make it someone else's fault.

But as long as we do that we reinforce the sin we have committed and prolong our guilt. We can't atone for our sin until we recognize it and come to terms with it.

That's what confession is. When we confess our guilt, we acknowledge the pain we have caused to ourselves and others.

Confession brings our guilt out of the dark places where we have hidden it into the light of conscious awareness. When we confess, we can experience the emotions we repressed. We can shed the tears we need to shed. We can look into the eyes of the people we have hurt. We can apologize. Our tears and their tears can flow into the same river.

Remember, we cannot be mistake free. Transgression will happen, either intentionally or unintentionally. And when it does we will have to come to terms with it. Every error must be corrected or it will hold us hostage.

Not many people understand the mechanism of guilt. Guilt is the psychological "pull back" or undertow that results from a sinful action. It is the effect of that action on our own consciousness. We may be aware of our guilt or we may repress it or deny it. But whenever we act in a way that hurts ourselves or others, that guilt remains somewhere in our psyche. It stays there even when we try to give it to someone else. In fact, the more we try to give our guilt to someone else the more deeply and firmly it becomes entrenched within our own consciousness.

We attempt to give our guilt to others because we are afraid we will be rejected by them if we admit our errors. Ironically, the opposite is true. Admitting our errors creates intimacy between us and other people. Not admitting our errors and trying to hide our guilt pushes others away and inevitably results in separation.

Rather than acknowledge our mistakes—which would give others the opportunity to forgive us for any hurt we have caused and restore a sense of connection between us— we choose to blame others for our errors, which of course only deepens the emotional chasm between us.

All this results from our fear. We are afraid to face the anger or hurt of others. We would rather pretend that there isn't any anger or hurt there to deal with. So we pretend to be innocent. "I didn't do anything here. If anybody did anything it was you, not me." Of course, anyone who knows reverse psychology understands that this denial on our part is practically a confession of our guilt.

Unfortunately, it is not a direct confession. It is a cowardly attempt to blame others for our mistakes. It is "story" time.

We think that if we can get others to believe our story, then we don't have to deal with the hurt or anger. And we can take our guilt and bury it somewhere where no one will notice it.

If we are successful, we will spend a great deal of our time and energy hiding the truth and upholding the deception. Indeed, if we do this long enough, we might even lose track of what the truth is.

Indeed, hiding our guilt seems to be an effective strategy for denying our feelings and those of others. However, its effectiveness is temporary. It works only for a while, because hidden guilt eventually rises to the surface, forcing us to acknowledge what we have tried so hard to hide.

Often it rises up with a vengeance, derailing our plans and exploding our carefully crafted self-image. When we see the damage report, we realize that we would have been better off facing the truth earlier on.

When all is said and done, repressing our guilt is not a strategy that contributes to our awakening. Indeed, it prevents us from using the natural function of our guilt as a tool for correction and atonement.

Once we see this clearly, we can begin to face our feelings and those of others more honestly. We can acknowledge our mistakes and the guilt that naturally arises from them.

Experiencing our guilt requires complete honesty, first

with ourselves and then with others. That honesty frees us from the exhausting compulsion to hide the truth. It enables us to drop our disguises and come clean.

Of course, in so doing, we may have to face the feelings of people we have injured. We may have to experience their anger, their grief, and their judgments. We might have to humble ourselves and ask for their forgiveness, but that is the beginning of our atonement.

Feeling the pain we have caused to ourselves and others is necessary if we are going to really experience our guilt and move through it. We must feel genuine remorse for our mistaken actions. Half-hearted efforts do not work here. There can be no more pretense, no more lying, to ourselves or to others.

The atonement process is an attempt to "make right" what went wrong. It is an attempt to be responsible when we have been irresponsible. Where possible, efforts to make amends or restitution toward our victims help us atone.

In the process, others may forgive us, or they may not. However, regardless of whether others forgive us, we cannot complete our atonement without forgiving ourselves.

A TRIUNE PROCESS

These are the three phases in the process of redemption. The first phase is Sin. Sin represents a thought or action that is wrong. It hurts us or it hurts others. When we commit a sin, we make a mistake.

The second phase in the process of redemption is Guilt.

Guilt is our awareness of the hurt we have caused to ourselves or others.

The third phase in the process of redemption is Atonement. Atonement is the correction and forgiveness of our mistake. It is the decision to accept responsibility for what we have done, to make amends where possible, and to learn from our mistakes so that we do not repeat them.

Just as Sin has no purpose if it does not induce Guilt, so Guilt has no purpose if it does not lead to Atonement. All three phases of the process of redemption must be experienced if transformation is to occur.

3

IMPERFECTION

God becomes as we are
that we may be as He is.
WILLIAM BLAKE

We believe that God is perfect and we want to be as God is. We don't want to make mistakes. How can we be children of God and make mistakes?

No matter how far we move into our freedom, this question keeps coming back. We expect to be perfect, even though it is quite obvious that perfection is not possible in the world we live in.

That is the set up. That is why Jesus was put on a cross. That is why we continue to crucify one another.

I want you to do it "right" and you want me to do it "right." But your idea of "right" and my idea of "right" do not match. You believe that ice cream should be eaten soft. I believe it should be eaten hard.

Right for you means the house is at least 75 degrees. Right for me means the thermostat is set at 65. This goes on forever. Neither you nor I nor anyone else can agree on what is "right."

In Israel, the Jews think that they are right and the Palestinians are wrong. The Palestinians don't agree.

You see, we humans cannot possibly be perfect, because even if it were possible for us to achieve perfection, it would be very unlikely that we would agree on what it is.

Ours is a world of beliefs and opinions. It is a world of subjective agendas, not of moral absolutes.

What is right? What constitutes perfection?

We would like to come to a consensus and, at times, it seems that we come close. But no matter how skillful we are as politicians, there is always some group, the needs of which we have not taken into account.

In the sixties, The Rolling Stones wrote a song called "you can't get no satisfaction." A lot of people identified with it.

Life doesn't come to us on our terms. Our ego cannot dictate what happens all the time. Sometimes we have to move out of our seat and let someone else sit down.

It isn't very pleasant, but life keeps asking us to be a little more patient and more humble than we are. Perhaps that is because if there is such a thing as "perfection" it won't be what our egos expect it to be. If there is some ultimate satisfaction that is possible for all of us, it might not present itself in the form of immediate need gratification.

Being "right" might have something to do with not making anyone else "wrong." Being "perfect" might have something to do with not demanding perfection.

You and I and everyone else on the planet might have to learn something to discover the potential for perfection that exists in our lives. We might have to grow, adjust, transform to come back into alignment with the divine will. Indeed, we might have to be mistaken about ourselves and others to learn what our true identity is.

Perfectionism is a human agenda, not a divine one. God accepts us as we are, mistakes and all. Unfortunately, we don't do the same for each other.

God is patient with us. He lets us make mistakes and learn from them. He has faith that we will learn eventually.

But we are impatient with each other. We think the other person will never get it.

What does that say about us? Who is the one up there on the cross taking the nails?

It isn't the person we judge. It is the one who is judging.

Judging or finding fault with others does not improve the quality of our lives. That's a spiritual truth that each one of us must discover for ourselves. No matter how hard we try, we cannot raise ourselves up by putting someone else down. Any advantage we gain through selfish behavior is illusory. But we aren't going to take someone else's word for it. We are going to have to find this out through our own experience.

The set up is ironic and paradoxical, of course. We find perfection only by accepting imperfection. We avoid making future mistakes only by accepting and learning from the mistakes we have already made.

The potential for perfection exists in each one of us, but it is not a worldly perfection. It is a perfection of the Spirit. We don't realize it by striving to be mistake free, but by having the courage to acknowledge our mistakes and learn from them.

Jesus did not come here to teach us not to sin. He came

here to teach forgiveness of sin. He did not say "do not trespass." He said "forgive us our trespasses."

The challenge of our post-Garden experience is to stop playing God and learn to be human; to stop expecting perfection and acknowledge our mistakes; to be humble, be patient, be teachable, be gentle with ourselves and others.

The God of Jesus is not a strict, unbending authority figure like the God of Abraham who punishes his children for their mistakes, but a forgiving and compassionate parent who lets his children make mistakes so that they can learn and evolve. Indeed, with the advent of Jesus' ministry, forgiveness is no longer some blessing that comes only from God. It is a blessing that we are asked to give each other. And by learning to give it to each other, we begin to learn to give it to ourselves.

Each one of us needs understanding, not condemnation. We need support, not blame. We need forgiveness, not retribution.

Do we want to live in a gentle world or a harsh one? There is no doubt that harsh, unforgiving actions lead to a world of fear and retribution. If we want a gentle world, we must learn to be gentle with each other.

That is the choice we were given when we claimed our freedom and it is the choice that stands before us now. We can keep looking over our shoulder hoping that God will intervene and fix things for us. But that is a bit naïve. If he did not intervene for Jesus on the cross or for the six million Jews that perished in Hitler's inferno, is He going to intervene now?

I'm afraid the decision is ours, not His. This post-Garden

world was not created by Him but by us. And we will have to learn to take responsibility for our creation and bring it back on track, or reap the consequences of our own irresponsible acts.

KARMA

In the blueprint of creation, learning from our mistakes is likely, but not guaranteed. We have to want to learn.

If we are willing to learn, we will eventually understand our errors and bring ourselves back on track. Remember, our mistakes do not condemn us.

What condemns us, so to speak, is our unwillingness to learn from our errors. If we are unwilling to admit that we are capable of making a mistake, or if we see our mistake but refuse to acknowledge it, then correction will not be possible. Without correction, we will continue to make the same mistake over and over. That is the law of karma.

Every mistake we make has certain consequences, not just for others, but for ourselves too. If correction is made promptly, those consequences can be minimized or even undone. Otherwise, we will continue to make the same mistake and the consequences will likely intensify.

When we are unwilling to bring our awareness to a mistake, events and circumstances are brought into being that force us to look at our actions and the suffering they have caused. These events and circumstances are attracted into our energy field by our unconscious guilt.

Sometimes it may seem to us that we are being punished

for our mistakes. But in truth karma and the pain associated with it does not punish us, but instead brings our guilt into conscious awareness. When we accept this invitation for honesty and face our guilt personally and interpersonally, the pain often subsides and the opportunity to atone for our error presents itself.

Guilt and Karma work hand in hand to raise our consciousness about our mistakes. When we face our guilt, the karmic consequences are minimal. But when we deny or project our guilt, the karmic consequences intensify. The law of karma makes it impossible for us to hide our guilt. Sooner or later, we will come to terms with our guilt and understand the consequences of our actions.

In some cases, we may be able to work through our guilt and atone for our major mistakes in this lifetime. Even when we resist being honest at first, life may eventually present us with a great opportunity for healing and forgiveness. In other cases, when our willingness to learn is weak, our guilt may stay submerged and we not face our karma in this life.

What we don't face here and now must eventually be faced at another time somewhere else. While everybody has a different idea of what the next life is or will be, what it is clear is that we take our unresolved guilt with us.

The lessons that we don't learn in this life will have to be learned in the next, whatever form that life takes. It is not necessary to speculate on the form to understand the content. And the content is what is critical here.

KARMA IS CONSEQUENCE

M any people think that Karma is punishment for our sins. That is because they do not understand that sin is an inextricable part of the trinity of redemption. We sin because we need to learn and we cannot learn without making mistakes.

If we are punished for our mistakes, we may decide to tow the line and do what the authority figures in our life want. Punishment can be effective behavior modification tool, but it does not often change our hearts. It doesn't guarantee that we will not make the same mistake again.

Only a compassionate and remorseful heart can change our patterns of projection and help us learn to take responsibility for the mistakes we would blame on others. Only a genuine willingness to face our guilt head on and atone for our actions breaks the cycle of violence and makes real change possible.

Karmic law brings events and circumstances into our lives not to punish us, but to wake us up, to help us acknowledge our mistakes and our guilt about them. Divine law inevitably asks us to take responsibility where we have refused to do so in the past. It asks us to break through our narrowness, our ignorance, and our deception to face the truth about ourselves.

It tells the Children of Adam and Eve that they cannot hide their creative power. That is not an option. Instead, they must learn to use this power responsibly.

Karma simply means the effects of our thoughts and

actions. In that sense, our loving thoughts and actions prosper. They have a positive, healing effect. We call that grace. Conversely, our unloving thoughts and actions create all kinds of stresses and difficulties in our lives. We call that suffering.

The law of karma operates all the time. Certain actions result in harmony and ease. Others result in disharmony and dis-ease. Just as harmony and ease manifest on all levels—physical, emotional, mental and spiritual—disharmony and dis-ease manifest also on all levels.

So you can see, we are not punished per say for acting in a sinful or irresponsible manner, but we are definitely asked to become accountable for our actions. When we decide to take responsibility for our actions, negative karmic conditions may lessen or even dissolve, Or they may lesson on certain levels, but not on others.

What is clear is that the more hurtful our mistakes are and the longer we have refused to learn from them, the more energetic and persistent our suffering must become in order to hold a strong enough mirror up to us. In cases where we hurt others intentionally, it may be necessary that we suffer in a similar way in order to awaken to the depth of our error and feel compassion for our victims.

That is where the concept of "an eye for an eye, a tooth for a tooth" comes from. However, this concept represents a spiritual law, not a human one. It applies only in the most egregious cases, in which a person has refused numerous opportunities to come to terms with the suffering s/he is causing. Unfortunately, the concept has been mistakenly used as a yardstick to mete out the punishment of one human being by another.

Human beings were never asked to take over the administration of divine justice. To the extent that they try, they simply create more suffering.

Divine justice (karma) operates throughout all of human experience. It is objective and impersonal. It is precise in determining the degree to which a person feels remorse and is willing to learn from his or her mistakes. Even Solomon with all his wisdom could not be so accurate, not to mention the many other human beings who propose to judge their brothers and sisters.

Some may escape human justice, but no one escapes divine justice. All of us are held to account for our thoughts and actions. That is not because God wants to punish us. It is because God wants us to learn to create responsibly. He wants us to learn to express ourselves without hurting or taking advantage of others.

These are the laws that apply to the post-Garden experience. And we learn how these laws function experientially. We create and then we see the effect of our creations on ourselves and others.

We may try to avoid divine justice by engaging in denial and projection, but this won't work forever. We may build our defenses high to hide our guilty secrets, but in the end all we succeed in doing is blocking out the love that we want.

Only those who have moved over the edge choose to live without love. They are condemned by their own choice. No one else has to punish them.

Yet even these hardened souls are free to make a different choice. When the knock comes on the door, they can answer the call honestly. They can admit that they are sick of carrying their guilt around, and they can confess, take responsibility for their actions, and ask for forgiveness.

When the door to truth is open, karmic conditions begin to shift. After all, divine law exists only to help us wake up, not to punish us. When we are willing to learn from our mistakes and take responsibility for our actions, we begin to come back into alignment with God's will. And what we bring into our lives is different when we begin working with the laws of God instead of against them.

4

CORRECTION OR PUNISHMENT

The new life would not be given him for nothing.
He would have to pay dearly for it,
but that is the beginning of a new story—
the story of his regeneration . . .
his initiation into a new unknown life.

FYODOR DOSTOEVSKY

We live with an erroneous assumption that punishing those who sin prevents them from sinning again. Statistics show that this is hardly the case. Punishing criminals without doing anything to foster their rehabilitation is tantamount to locking them up and throwing away the key.

That may suit some people fine, especially when criminals are in prison for life. But most people behind bars get out of prison. And, if we have done nothing to help them face their guilt and atone for their crimes, they come back into society with the same consciousness they had before being sentenced.

The price that we pay for not rehabilitating prisoners who will reenter society is a very high price. More often than not, it results in more crime and victims of crime.

Even prisoners who are locked away for life place a heavy financial burden on taxpayers. Efforts to help them lead more responsible and productive lives behind bars can save taxpayers money and give inmates an opportunity to change.

Does punishment ever help people change? Well, in certain rare cases it might help the person being punished to connect with his guilt. However, in most cases, it just reinforces his bitterness and victim consciousness. Often, it actually interferes with his natural willingness to feel his guilt and begin to take responsibility for what he has done.

Instead of punishing the criminal for not being responsible in the past, we may need to challenge him to take more responsibility for his actions now and in the future. Without offering the carrot, the use of the stick becomes utterly ineffective and meaningless. Without offering the criminal hope, how can we expect him to take responsibility?

REHABILITATION

An enlightened society encourages people to learn from their mistakes and redeem themselves. It also protects its members from people who continue to disregard the well-being of others.

While it may occasionally resort to punishment or imprisonment, its goal must always be to redeem and rehabilitate. It is a fact of life that not all will choose to learn from their mistakes. But it is also a fact of life that many whom we think are lost will find some desire to live and to learn that we never could have predicted.

To believe in the potential of people to transform themselves does not require any of us to be stupid or to deny the reality around us. We need to insist on proof of rehabilitation before allowing criminals back on the streets. Shutting our eyes and crossing our fingers as we watch inmates re-enter society is not good enough. They must be psychologically and spiritually ready and support mechanisms (jobs, counseling, appropriate housing) must be in place. And, even with all this, we need to keep both our eyes and our hearts open.

We are all looking for justice. The question we must ask is "What serves justice best: to demand an 'eye for an eye' or to correct the vision of the one who sees in error?"

If you believe that people cannot change you will choose the first strategy. If you believe that transformation is possible, you will choose the second one.

However, even if you favor the second strategy, you must be realistic. True redemption is a rigorous process. There is nothing soft or naïve about it. It requires that each person look at his mistake until he can acknowledge it. It requires that he sees and feels sorry for the pain that he has caused. And it requires that he is willing to make amends and learn from his mistakes.

Will every mistaken person learn from his mistakes just because we offer him the opportunity? Certainly not. It will be up to him to decide if he wants to learn. But that is a choice that each one of us makes moment to moment. It is not just a choice for the man or woman behind bars.

JUSTICE OR INJUSTICE

J ustice is the goal of our legal system and our criminal justice system. Yet, it is clear that justice is far more elusive than we think.

Not only do we condemn innocent people to imprisonment and death, we also do very little to rehabilitate the inmates in our prisons. As a result, we have an astronomically high recidivism rate. That means that well over half of the people who go to jail a first time return to prison after they have been released.

Our prisons create a culture that generates career criminals. To be sure, they have to work with the most difficult people. It isn't an easy task.

The problem lies not just with the competence of the people administering the system and providing its services. It is imbedded in the design of the system itself and the goals that it aspires to achieve.

The goal of the system is not to rehabilitate, but to punish. It is not to change hearts and minds but to make inmates "do time." Inmates are not asked to face their guilt, to confront their victims' anger, to take responsibility for their actions. No, they are simply locked up and dealt with on a custodial basis.

That does not mean that individuals who are motivated cannot find help. They can and they do. But these are the people who are going to turn their lives around anyway, with or without a therapeutic process.

However, the vast majority of prison inmates need a therapeutic process that will help them face their guilt and take responsibility for their actions. They aren't going to ask for this process. But they will take what we give them. And what we offer them right now is time and a culture as dire as the one they experienced on the streets.

How is justice served if there is little opportunity for criminals to transform their consciousness and their lives? Society does not want rapists, murderers and drug dealers back on the street, but this is what it is going to get if it continues to support a system based on punishment instead of rehabilitation.

Both on the individual and the collective level, we must understand the cycle of sin, guilt and atonement and support an approach to transgression that helps people go through all three phases of the cycle. Punishment prevents this from happening by short circuiting the process. As soon as we declare someone's guilt, we prescribe punishment as an atonement strategy. We say that we are satisfied if inmates do their time and we think that simply by doing it they will "pay their debt to society."

Well, sorry, folks. The debt to society is not paid. It is not even acknowledged. We think that if we put people in jail they will accept their guilt, but most of them don't. They justify their actions. They blame others. They pretend to be victims. But, for the most part, they don't face their guilt or admit their mistakes. They don't understand the suffering they have caused others. Or, if they do, they don't care.

They are not honest with themselves or with others. No foundation for change is built. When they leave prison, they do so with the same operating system that was in place when they committed their crimes.

If we want the streets of our communities to be safe, we have to insist that inmates leave prison with a different operating system than the one they had going in. That is going to take a lot of time and energy. It is going to take skillful rehabilitation staff who aren't easily manipulated or fooled. It's going to take reformed ex-inmates acting as role models. It is going to take confrontation, caring and lots of patience.

It is going to be a major investment for all of us. But the importance of this should not be underestimated. If we can learn to deal humanely and effectively with our worst sinners, then we can create a society where people can learn from their mistakes and improve their lives.

In a sense, our prisons are a microcosm of the society we live in. They reflect our values and our commitments. That should be a sobering realization for all of us.

How do we achieve justice? By punishing transgressors so that we and they can avoid dealing with guilt? No. We face our guilt and help them face theirs.

We offer strategies for telling the truth, opportunities for taking responsibility, expressing remorse, making amends or restitution. We look at sin not as a two part process the ends with punishment, but as a three part process that acknowledges the deepest levels of guilt and remorse and moves through a variety of atonement strategies toward healing and correction.

HEALING AND CORRECTION

There is no healing without correction. And there can be no correction without our willingness to learn from our mistakes.

Atonement doesn't happen without a change in heart. It is that change of heart that ultimately leads to a change in behavior. While it would be nice to think that this could happen overnight, it rarely does.

Fortunately, the one thing inmates have is plenty of time. The question is whether or not we are going to ask them to do something productive with that time.

To be sure, if we ask more of them, we are also going to have to ask more of ourselves. It is easier and probably cheaper to hire prison guards than it is to hire trained, street-wise therapists. It is easier to ask prisoners to "do time" than it is to ask them to be accountable for how they spend their time. But if we do not begin asking them to be accountable for their time in prison, how are they going to learn to be accountable when they get out? If we do not ask them to start acknowledging their mistakes and learning from them, how are they going to learn to stop blaming other people for their mistakes and attacking them?

Prisoners have a lot to learn. They could use a lot of their prison time learning to take responsibility for their thoughts, feelings and actions. They could learn appropriate boundaries. They could learn how to apologize to others, how to make amends when they have injured someone, and how to give and receive forgiveness. Do we really think that there is something better than this for them to do?

By not offering our best to them, we only cheat ourselves. They may be our prisoners for a few years. But if we don't use that time to help them change their hearts and minds, it is only a matter of time before the roles reverse and they come knocking at our doors. And then who will the prisoner be?

If we want our communities to be safe places, we have a lot of work to do. Prisons cannot be places where criminals are banished away from our oversight and allowed to maintain their culture of denial, projection, attack and retribution. We must step in and tear down those walls of denial. We must insist on truth telling and transparency. We must create an environment where guilt can be faced, not hidden or avoided.

We want criminals to feel their guilt and bring it out in the open, instead of finding a scapegoat and projecting their guilt onto him or her. We want to hear their confessions and expressions of remorse, for only then do we know that they are moving toward correction/atonement.

Through constant practice, deeply ingrained patterns of denial and avoidance of responsibility can be gradually broken and new, more responsible patterns set in motion. Friends and family can see that inmates are changing for the better and support them, even when they make mistakes.

Like Alcoholics in the AA program—and many offenders are also addicts of one kind or another—they must be encouraged to take one day at a time. Practice and patience are essential if they are going to be able to overturn old destructive patterns.

THE ROLE OF GROUPS

When people have similar lessons to learn, groups can be helpful in raising the consciousness of their members. Twelve Step or Affinity Groups that encourage people to confess their mistakes in an environment that is loving and accepting are powerful tools in the atonement process.

While many people benefit from the support of a "spiritual family" in cultivating healthy values and behavior, others must be careful that their search for acceptance does not result in their giving their power away to others who would like to control them. Indeed, some people commit crimes by succumbing to peer pressure and, as a result, their consciousness can be raised only by learning to stand up for their own values in the face of pressure from others. A group with guidelines that uphold clear boundaries can help them learn how to stand up for their own values and beliefs.

Cults of any kind must be avoided, as they themselves are agents of trespass incapable of understanding or upholding appropriate boundaries. They do not teach or support the principle of individual responsibility. While they may offer emotional support initially, this support is usually short lived and followed by a number of mentally and emotionally manipulative tactics designed to break down the self-esteem of members so that they surrender to the authority structure of the group.

Clearly, groups are powerful and can be tools for either atonement or trespass. However, as long as inmates take responsibility and refuse to give their power away, support groups can help them "anchor in" new values and behavior. Prisoners who have no hope or self-confidence can realize that they have the same power that they see reflected in the behavior of their sponsors or mentors. They can learn to have a new vision of who they are and what is possible for them.

BUILDING A CULTURE OF ATONEMENT

Working with prisoners keeps us from becoming too romantic about the concept of atonement. We can't help but be humbled by the tremendous challenge of helping some of the most angry people on the planet move from distrust to trust, from denial to responsibility. Yet we know that unless they can travel this rocky road to freedom, we won't be able to travel it either. For the only difference between those inside the prison walls and those outside them is one of degree.

We all left the same Garden and we have the same story. They just chose to dramatize that story more than we did. Prison became their metaphor for exile. And because they are our brothers and sisters, it is our metaphor too. They may reflect the pain of exile with a greater intensity than we do, but it is the same pain.

Building a culture that supports atonement is both their work and ours. It is both individual work and collective work. It asks each one of us to take personal responsibility for facing our guilt and atoning for our mistakes. And it also asks us to work together to build a society that encourages honesty and responsibility from all of its members.

Regardless of which side of the prison walls we inhabit, we have the same work to do. We need to take down the walls of fear that keep us in denial. We need to have the courage to admit our mistakes and to stop blaming each other for them. We need to work hard to build a culture in which mistakes are perceived not as opportunities for ridiculing or condemning each other, but as opportunities to see our weaknesses and strengthen them.

Because they are in prison, and their anger, their pain and their denial is pervasive and profound, we cannot approach this task in a naïve fashion. We can't ask for too much at first or we will fail. We have to start with the basics. We have to start with the bar fairly close to the ground.

If a child is three feet tall and we set the bar at two feet, he will not be able to jump over it. He is bound to fail. But if we set the bar at 6 inches and keep raising it as he grows, it will not be that long before he can hurdle the two feet we expect from him.

Everyone has the capacity to improve. Even criminals can become more skillful, more compassionate, more responsible, more honest, more loving. They can learn to acknowledge their pain and face their guilt.

It won't be easy. It won't be quick. But with persistence and patience it can happen. Our goal may be redemption, but we will need to take baby steps toward it. We will have to deal with where we are today, not with where we would like to be in the future.

We are not rebuilding the culture of pretense and denial, after all. We are building a new culture based on honesty and willingness to learn.

It is a different culture than any we have known. And it will be a challenge to build it on our planet, in our countries, our communities, our families, indeed in our own hearts and minds. But it is the great work we came here to do. It is the Garden we must build, not because we have been abandoned by God, but because the God's light and God's love went with us into the three dimensional world. And it is by finding and reclaiming that light and that love that we understand the truth about ourselves and our mission here.

For we are master builders all. We have entered an imperfect world to discover that perfection does not lie outside of us, nor does it lie within our ego structure. If perfection exists, it exists in the blueprint of our evolution. It exists in our willingness to learn, to adapt, to grow and transform.

When God gave us the key to the Garden gate, He told us that we could come back home when we were ready. What we did not know is that the Garden of Eden was not a physical place, but a place of peace within our hearts and minds. We can find that place even if we are in prison.

Without the possibility for redemption this experiment in freedom is and will continue to be a rather grim affair. God knew this and He reminded us that the Key to the Garden gate worked both ways.

When we re-enter the Garden, we do so with a consciousness that is different from the one with which we left. We "return" having moved from ignorance to knowledge, back to grace. We return as conscious beings who create and take responsibility for our creations.

We may return to the same place where we started, but we are not the same. We have learned to be a little more gentle and compassionate. We have learned to forgive ourselves and each other.

5

LIGHT IN THE DARK PLACES

I have heard the mermaids singing each to each.
I do not think that they will sing to me.

T.S. ELLIOT

In Greek Mythology, Erebus is the place of deepest darkness. It is the underground world where chaos reigns. In modern psychological terms, Erebus represents the shadow world of our unconscious. In this world, dreams and symbols reign. It is the place where death dwells and it is also the place where life is conceived. Indeed, it is said that, in the earliest of time, Erebus and Nyx (Night) dwelled in love, and that Hermera (Day) and Aether (Light) were born from them.

From a spiritual standpoint, Erebus is the place of mysteries and beginnings. From it arises psychic dreams, revelations, and intuitions of truth which are beyond our understanding. Wisdom that comes from this place does not originate in our conscious minds. It comes from the unconscious or superconscious.

The world of darkness represents both our ignorance and the source of our greatest illumination. In that sense it is a dichotomous world. It is a world that we do not understand very well. Yet, we know that without this world, there would be no creativity, no random beauty, no serendipity. There would be only logic, symmetry, and causal order.

The emotion of love itself would not exist. For love is as much a creation of the darkness as it is of the light. Love is not just beautiful, intentional and uplifting. It is needy, sudden and compelling. It is both gradual and unpredictable, safe and dangerous, lawful and illicit.

Like our unconscious, Erebus is a complex, rich, dynamic place. It is a place where duality and unity exist side by side. It is not, nor will it ever be, one-dimensional.

Erebus is a hidden world. There is a lot going on there, but we don't know very much about it. In order to understand the mysteries of this world, we have to look and listen deeply. We can't be preoccupied with the outer world. We have to go within.

A DIFFERENT FORBIDDEN FRUIT

The myth of Persephone offers us a different perspective on guilt, sin and atonement. In some ways, it might be more accurate psychologically than the myth of Adam and Eve and the Serpent in the Garden.

According to the myth, Zeus gives his brother Hades permission to abduct his daughter Persephone. Hades rises up from a dark hole in the earth right next to where Persephone is plucking and gathering narcissus in a flowery meadow. He seizes Persephone and takes her off to the underworld. Persephone resists and asks both gods and men for help, but because Hades has Zeus' permission nothing can be done to prevent the abduction. Finally, Demeter, Persephone's mother, appeals to Zeus with tears in her eyes and Zeus relents. He agrees to set Persephone free so long as she has not eaten any food in the underworld. However, by the time Hermes arrives in the underworld carrying Zeus' message, Persephone has already eaten half a pomegranate that Hades gave to her as an expression of love. Thus, Persephone's permanent return to upper world is no longer possible.

As a compromise, Persephone is allowed to spend six months with her mother in the upper world and then must return to the underworld for the rest of the year. Her descent to the underworld happens in the fall and her ascent to the upper world happens in the spring.

The cyclical nature of this journey to and from the underworld is more reflective of the circular nature of the process of sin and redemption than is the biblical myth of the Fall. It is also more psychologically profound.

While the myth of the fall focuses on the expulsion from the garden, little is said about the return journey or the process by which we integrate knowledge and atone for our mistakes. The story of Persephone is more explicit. She must spend half of her life in the underworld, the world of the unconscious, where chaos and darkness reign. She enters the underworld just before winter comes to the earth, when light is approaching its lowest point and many living things become dormant.

Unlike the outer world which has slowed down and is resting, the inner world is experiencing its greatest creativity. The branches of the tree may be empty of leaves, but the roots are reaching deep into the earth for nurturing.

Persephone's journey is an inner one. It is an exploration of her own unconscious and the collective unconscious of all human beings. It is a journey that enables her to gain some insight into the shadowy world of dreams and impulses, so that she can bring this insight forward into conscious understanding. Every spring she emerges from the underworld into the upper world.

It is not coincidental that she emerges as the seeds sprout and break through the earth. Her entry into the upper world signals the most creative time in that world. Flowers are blooming. Leaves are turning the bare trees green. It is a time of rebirth.

The psychological clarity of the Persephone story helps us understand that the myth of the fall is incomplete. It needs another part that focuses on the movement toward grace and redemption.

CIRCLES AND STRAIGHT LINES

Some may argue that the New Testament offers us the second part of the story—and it is certainly true that the teachings of Jesus provide us with a roadmap for redemption—but the Judeo-Christian story is still too linear to be psychologically helpful.

Persephone descends and ascends every year. Her journey could just as easily be tied to the monthly lunar cycle or the daily cycle of the earth's rotation on its axis. All of these cycles represent a movement from darkness to light and back to darkness.

The evolution of consciousness is more accurately portrayed in a cyclic fashion than in a linear one. We don't just move in a straight line from darkness to light or from ignorance to knowledge. We move in a crooked line. Or, to put it more clearly, the line is not straight, but curved. We wake up a little, then go to sleep and wake up again. We learn, then forget what we have learned, and then remember it.

We deny our guilt and then have to go looking for it. When we find it, we acknowledge and accept what we can, and we project the rest. We take a little responsibility and give the rest to someone else. We tell a little bit of the truth and hide the remainder.

Enlightenment doesn't happen all at once and it doesn't happen in a straight line. We keep recycling our lessons until they really sink in and then we move on to other ones. It is a cyclical process.

In the Christian model, once you accept Jesus, you are saved. There's no more work to do, except perhaps to run around trying to save others.

This is great if it works for you, but for most people it doesn't work very well. Jesus isn't going to save you or your mother from cancer, just as God didn't save him from the cross. And it's not because he doesn't love you.

It's because you volunteered to join this classroom and that means you have to stay for the lesson. No excuses. You can't refuse to take responsibility for learning to love more deeply. You can't avoid expanding your consciousness. It is why you are here.

And class meets every day, not just once or twice in your

life, even if you met Jesus or Buddha on that day. Class meets every day and you have to get up and go to school.

There is no spiritual awakening without spiritual practice. Both Jesus and Buddha will tell you that.

There is no vicarious atonement. Each person has to atone for himself. Each person has to learn the lesson in his own time and place, even though we all may be learning similar lessons.

Spiritual communities support us in getting up for class, but they can't take the class for us. They can ring the bell at 4 AM every day, but we are the ones who have to get up and brush our teeth.

Of course, I know a few communities that will brush your teeth for you, but I'm not going to go there. Suffice it to say that they are the ones who believe that atonement happens in a straight line.

Anyway, most of us have to raise our own toothbrush if we want to have clean teeth. And, it may be a pain, but we get used to it.

When you are a little kid, your mother or father has to remind you to brush your teeth. But as you get older, you have to assume this responsibility.

Sure, there will be times when you forget or don't feel like it. But you won't stop brushing. You'll continue to brush, in your own way, in your own timeframe.

Whether that's once a week or three times a day is up to you. Regardless, your practice is cyclical. It is periodic. It is rhythmic.

The atonement process is the same way. You sin and you

catch it, or you don't. If you don't, you feel bad or you make someone mad and you get to look at it again. Maybe you see your mistake and you say "I'm sorry" or maybe you don't. And around and around it goes until you realize that you cannot attack anyone except yourself and you realize you don't want to do that anymore because it's too painful.

But then you do something else, or you say something else that pushes peoples' buttons, or they do or say something that pushes yours and you realize that your stuff is up again for inspection. And if you don't want to see it, someone eventually puts it right under your face.

And after a while of going into it and coming out of it, you begin to sympathize with poor Persephone, who is married to a guy she both loves and hates and has to report to a mother she isn't always keen on seeing.

And you realize it's all a drama of hide and seek, and the less you hide, the fewer upset people come looking for you.

Of course, I don't want to minimize or trivialize the learning process we are engaged in here by suggesting that it is all a big game. But most of us take it so seriously, we forget to be gentle with ourselves and each other.

So in the interests of safety and civility, we all need to "lighten up" a bit. Erebus is not as bad a place as it seems and we know that no matter how deep we descend, we will eventually come out into the light, just as Persephone does.

Or to use a more contemporary metaphor we need to keep our cool when we step up to the plate. That way we can take our best swings at the ball and still feel okay whether we strike out or hit a home run.

Sure it's always more fun to hit the ball out of the park than it is to hit a "nubber" to the pitcher's mound. It's always more pleasant to win than to lose the game, but either way we need to remember that "it's just a game." Winning does not make us "good." And losing does not make us "bad."

Each one of us will have our share of wins and losses. Each one of us will make our share of mistakes and faux pas. We'll learn from some and others will beat us over the head for years before we finally learn to take responsibility for our actions.

That's the way it is. That's the nature of the game.

We come here with a variety of virtues and skills. Some of us are more patient than others. Some are smarter, kinder, more capable or more focused. It doesn't matter. We all have to work with what we have.

Envying others or pitying them doesn't help. Neither an inferiority complex nor a superiority complex will make our lives any easier. Whether we think we are better than others or not as good, we're bound to meet people who will challenge our belief systems.

So the bottom line is: can we be a happy player? Can we do our best and know that whatever that is, it will be okay?

UNDERWORLDS

Sometimes we get very invested in the drama of our lives and, with that investment, comes a certain harshness of demeanor. We forget to be kind and compassionate toward ourselves and others. We play the game a little too aggressively.

Recently a Massachusetts father was convicted for killing his son's hockey coach during a dispute at hockey practice. Suddenly, the game was not just a game, but a fight to the death. Now one man is behind bars and the other one is dead. The children of both men will grow up without their fathers. When the game becomes too harsh, everyone loses.

At times like this, we all get a wake-up call. "Remember, it's just a game and it is impossible to play it without a certain measure of trust, fairness, and goodwill." When we lose our composure, not to mention our kindness, it is impossible to enjoy or make sense of the ups and downs of life.

We forget that there can be dignity not only in victory, but also in loss, especially when we give our best. You and I don't want to live in a world where we are condemned for our mistakes or shortcomings and our best is not enough. That would truly be a hell on earth.

God did not create such a world. Why should we? God gave us a world where we could learn to be responsible for our mistakes. Can we embrace this world and learn to care for it? Or will we insist on making a different world, a world empty of compassion, tolerance, and forgiveness?

In both the Judeo-Christian myth and the Greek myth, the choice was ours. We decided to eat the forbidden fruit. We wanted to take this responsibility.

Even though Persephone was abducted against her will, she took the pomegranate from Hades and ate it willingly. She could not refuse his love. She knew that learning to love was her raison d'etre and her destiny. And of course in order to learn of love she had to live part-time in the underworld.

Living in the underworld means exploring our unconscious drives and compulsions. It means experiencing our sexuality, our power, our anger, jealousy, greed, and so on. It means looking at the chaotic and untidy aspects of our consciousness.

If we do not take the time to do this, these unruly aspects of ourselves cannot become integrated into our conscious experience. So spending time in the underworld—unpleasant as it might seem—is an essential part of our spiritual path.

The journey to love has a lot to do with looking at the parts of ourselves that are unloving. Our goal must not be to hide our unloving thoughts and feelings, but to recognize them and confess them.

An integrated person is not afraid of her anger, her fear or her sexuality. For she has faced herself in the darkness and found the light within. When she moves now, both darkness and light move with her.

When Persephone descends into the underworld she brings the power of the light. She exposes those who would play the victim or blame others for their suffering. When she ascends into the upper world, she brings the power of the darkness and challenges those who fearfully cling to the light. With her help, they learn to find the parts of themselves they have tried to hide or avoid.

Her wholeness or spiritual completion comes from the synergy of dark and light, unconscious and conscious, ignorance and knowledge. It is both gentle and robust, creative and receptive, confident and humble.

Spiritual wholeness represents the reconciliation of the most high with the most low, the supreme oneness with the myriad manifestations. Its inner radiance is not threatened by darkness. Its love is not threatened by fear.

The true spiritual journey is not a desire to escape from life—no matter how rough or unsavory it seems—but to meet it with courage and honesty. It is not a journey of denial, but a journey of revelation.

Because we face our mistakes, we learn to correct them. Because we look at our prejudice and conceits, we overcome our ignorance and pride. Because we have the courage to see our resistance and controlling behavior, we learn to surrender and allow life to unfold.

It is precisely because we face the shadow that we discover the light. For darkness is nothing substantial, but merely the absence of the light.

When we are no longer afraid of our fear, it can have no power over us. Then we can walk with it and through it. And that is a sign that we have come to the end of our journey in the underworld.

When our descent into the underworld is complete, our ascent can begin. But those who try to ascend to the heights of heaven before they have learned to love and accept themselves will find themselves awash like J. Alfred Proofrock in the drawingrooms of hell.

Polite society is always thoroughly undermined by the ghosts and goblins of the unconscious. Like it or not, the demons we repress we must ultimately face. They may disappear for a while, but they won't go away.

And the mysterious voices we hear in the morning would not be there if we had not tossed and turned all night. We may escape them during the day, but the furies will find us at night. So better hold tight to the gunwale because the wind will howl, the waves will swell, and the boat will roll and shake.

We humans are here not just to learn the laws of physics, but to understand something about ourselves. And if we are going to do that, we must look deeply, without trying to hide all the things we don't like. That is a psychological and spiritual quest of the greatest proportions.

As we move down that road, we must face all of the sins, distortions and aberrations of the human psyche. Indeed, to choose what is good and right, we must see our capacity for evil. To know the truth, we must wrestle with our seemingly endless capacity to lie and deceive.

The tree of knowledge has very deep roots. Did we think we would get away with just exploring the branches?

Once we ate of the fruit, we committed ourselves to finding its origins. And that is a numinous, if not heroic, journey.

6

TERROR & CORPORATE GUILT

Things fall apart; the centre cannot hold;
Mere anarchy is loosed upon the world;
The blood-dimmed tide is loosed, and everywhere
The ceremony of innocence is drowned;
The best lack all conviction, while the worst
Are full of passionate intensity.

W.B. YEATS

It is interesting that the dominant culture and the greatest material power on earth is now being threatened by an enemy that practices deception and hides in caves deep underground. If we ever needed a more exacting metaphor for the world of the collective unconscious we would not find it.

These terrorists not only take the lives of innocent people; they also attack the very values on which we build our society. Their goal is to undermine and disrupt our social order using any means at their disposal.

It is certainly not surprising that we have no sympathy for these men. Yet, in our distaste for them and their extremely cruel behavior, we might dismiss an opportunity to look into the message their actions evoke from the dark depths of the collective psyche.

What is that message?

Before the attack on New York and Washington, most of us didn't care very much about the plight of the women and children of Afghanistan. We were isolated on the other side of the world. An ocean separated us from some of our friends and many of our enemies.

Now, after September 11, 2001, that ocean no longer separates us. We have become vulnerable. Like it or not, we have been forced to listen. We can no longer ignore the suffering of third world peoples, nor can we refuse to see how their suffering is manipulated by extremists with lethal terrorist agendas.

Something quintessential has changed. The paradigm has shifted.

Now, America is an engaged nation. People overseas aren't just eating our hamburgers and buying our CDs. They are buying or stealing our bombs, our missiles, our chemical and biological weapons, or those of our former enemies. These deadly products are now in the hands of people who don't have the moral restraint we or the Soviets exercised in the past.

The tables have been turned on us. It was bound to happen.

Just as the contents of the personal unconscious erupts and forces the individual to take notice, so the collective unconscious occasionally erupts and forces all of us to recognize and integrate its contents into our conscious awareness.

It would be easy to approach this eruption in the collective psyche in a purely military fashion. We have been attacked and so we will attack back and build better defenses against future attacks. Not that this strategy is entirely incorrect, but if it is our only strategy, we will have missed the lesson we are being asked to learn.

The third world is no longer happy being third. Poor nations want to develop their economies so that they can raise the standard of living of their people.

The developed world must loosen its grip on the resources of the world and share what it has with poorer nations. If it does not do this voluntarily, it will be compelled to do so through a variety of pressures that bubble up from the caldron of the collective unconscious. That is how integration and balance is achieved in a volatile world.

By not listening to the voices of people who are poor, hungry, sick and disenfranchised around the world, we create the conditions in which they will be receptive to the propaganda of our enemies. Why is Bin Laden such a sympathetic figure in the Islamic world? It is not because people approve of his tactics. It is not even because people agree with his moral, religious or political views. It is because they are poor and America is rich. It is because they fight with machine guns and suicide bombers and America fights with tanks, planes and missiles.

People who exist under conditions of poverty or oppression are more easily manipulated by pundits and terrorists who seek to blame rich nations for their plight. Why would such people resist the temptation to see America as the enemy? It would be too much to expect.

America has discovered fairly quickly that it must send food with its bombs if it is not to be hated by the people it seeks to liberate. The war we are waging will not be won in a military fashion. We must win people's hearts and minds. We must show people through our humanitarian efforts who we really are if we want them to overcome their stereotyped and distorted images of us. They must see our values in action, not just our army or our airplanes.

The destruction of the World Trade Center Towers by a small band of terrorist hijackers represents a "mushing" of the boundaries between third world and first world realities. It is a clear paradigm shift, empowering those who have very little and making the rich and powerful nations vulnerable. It is a sign of tremendous creative activity on the unconscious level and it evokes the need for social and economic strategies that will address the needs it brings to our attention.

This is not just an energetic phenomenon, but also a values crisis of the greatest proportions. People will no longer accept hypocrisy, empty rhetoric or political doublespeak. They want our actions to be consistent with our words and the values we profess to live by.

One hundred and fifty years ago, we fought a war in America to end the brutal practice of slavery. A poor and disenfranchised people was legitimized and gradually empowered and lifted up. This process has never been pretty or perfect, nor is it complete.

Nevertheless, what America did for its underclass who came to our shores against theirs wills—and what it has consistently done for poor immigrants who came here voluntarily—it must now help the world do for the underclass in all of its countries.

There are those in America who argue for our isolation and detachment from the affairs of the rest of the world. But in the face of the growing global economy and ongoing communications revolution, such a view is clearly anachronistic. It is also essentially at odds with our dynamic movement toward ever-increasing pluralism and diversity.

Whether we intended it or not, America has always been a melting pot. Because it citizens represent every race, every religion and every culture, it stands for assimilation and integration and against all forms of extremism, political or religious.

Both isolationism and imperialism are extremes our country must continue to avoid. Our goal must not be to impose our cultural norms and values on the people of any other nation. Indeed, any effort to do so will only support the Bin Ladens of this world and fuel the continued rise of international terrorism.

This is not an argument for an imperialist agenda. It is not an argument in support of any kind of missionary compulsion, religious or economic. It is not an argument for appropriation, but for inclusion.

With all of our problems and imperfections, America is still the most sought after home for refugees and immigrants seeking economic, religious or political freedom. We don't go out seeking converts to our way of life. It is not necessary. America grows through the principal of attraction. People like what we have to offer here. They are attracted to our way of life.

That does not mean that all people like us. Indeed, we see

now in no uncertain terms that some people around the world hate us and believe that our way of life is sinful. While it is true that our freedom may sometimes lead toward excess—and we may be judged for the indecency of those instances—curbing our freedom of self expression is not the answer. That is too high a price to pay for moderation.

It is true that having too much is obscene: too much money, too much food, too much drink, too much sex, too much violence on television, too many adult bookstores and so on. But if we vote to get rid of the things we consider obscene, what will stop the lords of censorship from taking away the expressions of freedom that we support or enjoy?

The truth is that what one person considers obscene someone else views as an inalienable right. And, as offended as some of us are by certain aspects of our culture, are we willing to let the government decide what newspapers or television programs are available to us?

We keep our country healthy by tolerating differences of opinion. We keep our religious freedom alive by separating the powers of church and state. We work hard at our commitment to the philosophy of inclusion. We not only preach it; we act on it every day of our lives.

That is why it was so easy for Bin Laden's terrorists to gain entrance to our country. We didn't use racial profiling to stop them from getting on the planes.

To increase their likelihood of success, these men were told to shave their beards and wear inconspicuous western clothing. They were encouraged to act like us. And, of course, that is what made them dangerous. They looked like us, but they had a very different agenda. They were wolves in sheep's clothing.

Now we think that just because we are making our grandmothers take off their shoes we are safe against another terrorist assault. Do we think the wolf will show up yet again dressed like a sheep?

We want to guarantee safety to our citizens, but we can't. There is no more safety.

The disenfranchised have risen up, albeit they have chosen the most unlikely of messengers. The collective unconscious is spewing forth its bottled up rage and civilization is reeling!

The old boundaries that protected us no longer work. The underworld is rising into the upper world. The third world is reaching into our living rooms, our pocket books and our hearts. And we are inextricably connected to that world, not just by trade and satellite technology, but by the spread of contagious diseases and the proliferation of terrorist networks.

We are coming to a time in human history when we are all beginning to realize the truth of the spiritual teaching that tells us that as long as one person in this world is not at peace, the world cannot be at peace. This is a time in which inclusion is the way, the truth, and the life. No one can be excluded any longer. The freedom that we want for ourselves we must be willing to share with all.

CANCER IN THE COLLECTIVE BODY

The recent attack by terrorist "cells" in the United States against highly symbolic economic, political and military targets can be compared to the attack of particularly virulent cancer cells on the major organ systems of the body. These cells may be tiny, but their potential to cause destruction is substantial and they need to be taken seriously.

There are two ways to deal with cancer. One is to try to kill it using radiation or chemotherapy. In Afghanistan, we are using cruise missiles and bunker bombs.

That strategy may kill a lot of the cancer cells, but it doesn't necessarily kill all of them. And it takes only a few cells to undermine the health of the body.

Our military campaign in Afghanistan has been successful by many standards. But there are still Al Qaeda soldiers hiding in the caves and the only way we can apprehend them is to go down into those caves and bring them out. That is a dangerous task. It means living right at the edge between life and death.

To win against cancer—in the individual and collective body—we must investigate its origin. We need to discover the root of this disease in our minds and bodies. We need to find out why and how the body is making these cancer cells. Then we can help the body stop making them.

Our struggle against terrorism must also go to the root of the problem. That root won't be found in a cave in Afghanistan, because Al Qaeda is not the cause, but the symptom of the dis-ease. The cause of the dis-ease is poverty, hunger, illiteracy and a religious fundamentalism that exploits these conditions to serve its own narrow ends. How many boys in Pakistan or Afghanistan would have been raised in fundamentalist Islamic schools if their parents could have given them another option? If we want these people to make different choices we must help them find alternatives. And those alternatives begin with food, proper housing, jobs and educational opportunities for their children.

Once we are aware that a normal cell has become cancerous, we must realize that the entire body is threatened. We must not only try to remove that cancerous cell, but offer other cells a different pathway.

I don't believe that the use of the term "terrorist cell" is a coincidence. For these people live among us. They might even be our neighbors.

We are calling this a war on terrorism, but that isn't a very accurate term, because terrorism is not the root cause of the problem. Are we going to be happy destroying the terrorists and their training camps or are we going to commit to addressing the ignorance, poverty and oppression that gives terrorism its foothold in Afghanistan and other countries?

These are not just questions for Americans but for all citizens of the world. Both terrorism and the economic/social/political environments that support it are global threats, not just national ones. They are threats that cannot be successfully addressed without the commitment of the world community.

It is ironic but true that the attack against the World

Trade Center claimed the lives of people from countries all over the world. It was an attack on New York City, not only the pride and joy of the America's melting pot, but the home of the United Nations. It was an attack on pluralism, tolerance, diversity, and freedom everywhere.

We may think that getting rid of Bin Laden or Al Qaeda will solve this problem, but that is self-deceptive thinking. The problem is not in Afghanistan, Middle Asia or even the Middle East. The problem is in our hearts and minds.

That is where we must remove our excesses and address the issue of obscenity. No one else can do it for us, not even our government. We must decide "how much is enough" for our health and well being and live within the boundaries of that choice. We must decide what our inalienable rights are and voluntarily let go of any opportunity to exploit others for our own benefit. The choice to act in harmony with self and other only has meaning when no one is holding a gun to our head.

We must take on the yoke of self-restraint. Only this choice, individually and collectively, will lead to responsible behavior while safeguarding our freedom.

In the end it is a moral and spiritual issue. It always comes down to that. It is a choice to see our errors and to learn from them.

The only change that is real is the one that is voluntary and comes from the understanding of our minds and the compassion of our hearts. And, in the end, we can decide only for ourselves. We cannot prescribe for others.

TAKING STOCK AND LOSING IT

The paradigm was already shifting when two planes carrying people slammed into the World Trade Center in New York City, bringing down the Twin Towers and killing thousands of innocent people. It was already shifting when another plane slammed into the Pentagon and a second plane meant for the Pentagon or the White House was forced to crash in a field in Pennsylvania.

In retrospect, we now know that—had the passengers of that second plane not acted to abort the mission of the terrorists on board—Airforce fighters would have shot the plane down, a grisly choice to say the least. A few months later, passengers and flight crew on an flight crossing the Atlantic acted to prevent another tragedy.

Ordinary people are fighting the new war. Citizens are being asked to stand up and help. And they are doing it.

Millions of Americans are donating money and blood and thousands of volunteers are helping to find victims under the rubble of the World Trade Center. Still others are ministering to the victims' families in one way or another.

The hearts of the American people have been touched. And we are reaching out to each other as never before.

Sometimes it takes a tragedy to bring out the best in us. Trespass is not just an expression of the Trespasser's beliefs and values. It is a wake up call for the one sustaining the attack. It mobilizes his inner resources, his resilience, his values.

Those who attack us call us to stand up for ourselves.

They force us to remember who we are and announce it to the world.

We may have been asleep at the helm when we were attacked, but now we are alert and our hand is on the tiller. Despite previous words of warning from experts on terrorism, we had been lulled into a false sense of security. But now, after 9/11, that sense of security does not exist.

Facing terrorism means facing our worst fears. It means looking into the darkest corners of the human psyche. Bin Laden may personify the face of evil in our time, but what he represents is not confined just to terrorists from the Arab world. He represents a part of all of us.

I know that we don't want to own this. We don't want to claim any common ground with Bin Laden. We want to make him radically different from us. We want and need to see him as an animal, not a human being. We want to depersonalize him, objectify him. We want to call him a demon or a devil, just as he and others from the Arab world call us the "Great Satan."

"Only a hideous, amoral, monster could perpetrate such an act," we want to believe. And yes, in a way, it is true. Bin Laden's actions do reflect his mentality, just as our actions reflect ours.

But there is a level of untruth in our perception. For Bin Laden is not just showing us himself. He is also showing us our own dark side.

If you don't believe this, then consider what has happened in the world in the last couple of months. The biggest news story since 9/11 is the Enron bankruptcy. Enron represents the dark side of capitalism. It personifies a system of commerce based on secrecy and disinformation where the common good is subverted by a small group of privileged executives and board members. Thousands of employees lost life savings, while a few individuals made a fortune.

Meanwhile, the executives of Enron have long tentacles that extend like perverse roots run amuck into the secret chambers of the White House and the Congress. Enron was a major corporate contributor to many of our politicians in power, including our President and Vice President.

The quid pro quo of Enron's contributions to our politicians seems to be the willingness of government regulators to turn a blind eye to the kind of abuses of employee and shareholder trust that have recently surfaced in the news. And in this case, blindness seems to be endemic to both political parties.

What kind of a message about capitalism or democracy does that send to the Arab World? Did we forget that just a year ago our country was having a hard time determining whom it elected to the presidency because of flaws in ballot design, vote counting procedures and other unquestioned aspects of the political process.

One would have thought such a fiasco would have made it crystal clear to Americans how important it was to enact campaign finance reform and other measures designed to insure fair elections and access to the political process for all citizens. But it seems that the country needed a more compelling example to begin to pay attention to this issue.

Since 9/11, the economy has suffered. Jobs have been

lost. Investors have become jittery. We have been hovering on the brink of a recession. And just when the economy begins to show some signs of recovery, the Enron scandal erupts from the caldron of the collective psyche.

It was not a plane hitting a building. But it was a kind of corporate terrorism. Thousands of people lost their jobs and their life savings.

Collective guilt, like individual guilt, must surface in order for it to be acknowledged. Secrets must be told. Corporate denials must be unmasked for the lies they are. There must be no more pretense, no more cover up.

And atonement—if it is to happen—requires that people admit their mistakes and take responsibility for their actions. An atonement strategy must be in place to right the wrongs that were done. People who lost life savings need to be reimbursed.

All that goes without saying, although there should be more of us saying it. But the irony is that Enron erupts on the screen of the collective consciousness exactly when our president is gloating over the military success in Afghanistan and touting the triumph of American values and democracy.

I'm not saying that we don't have reason to celebrate who we are or the values that have been reawakened in us since 9/11. There is much for us to be proud of as Americans. But the Enron affair underscores that there is also a lot for us to look at.

America has a dark side. And we will not defeat terrorism unless we have the courage to look at it. Like Persephone, we must journey back and forth between the upper world and the lower world if we are to learn the meaning of the word "freedom" or the word "love."

The lens through which America looks is not spotless. There are stains that need to be recognized and cleaned up. The values we preach and profess are not always the ones that we express in our homes or in our companies. We cannot hold ourselves up as a model to the world of economic freedom and democracy if we create a haven for companies who exploit their employees and manipulate our elected politicians to serve their corporate agendas.

Before we start to gloat, Mr. President, we need to clean up our act. It is always tempting to act "holier than thou." But I'm afraid that this is just a mindless imitation of the behavior of our enemy. We are not the "great infidel," as our enemy sees us, but our economic and political institutions are not untarnished either. We have a lot of work to do before we hold ourselves up as a model for others.

This is not a one dimensional struggle. We are not just waging war with an outer enemy, but with an inner one as well. Ben Laden is not just hiding in Afghanistan or Pakistan; he is hiding in our hearts.

If you doubt that and believe in our absolute moral superiority over our enemy, just visit the corporate boardrooms of the Fortune 500 companies. If you could videotape a few of the conversations that take place in those places, you might find them just as incriminating as the Bin Laden tape we found in his safe house in Afghanistan.

I don't think there are any more safe houses, here or in Afghanistan. Wherever the truth is hidden or stored away, it will be discovered and revealed. All the information will get out.

Some of it will be good news. Some of it will not. And we, as citizens of our country and as citizens of the world, will have to look at all of it, like it or not.

That is the beauty of truth. Sometimes it lurks in dark and unseemly places. And sometimes it explodes right in front of us like a burning bush.

7

MOVING OUT OF DENIAL

First, we see through a glass darkly,
and then face to face.

CORINTHIANS

E nron and other For-Profit Corporations are not the only organizations with guilty secrets. Many Non-Profit Organizations, including some of the biggest ones, often have dark secrets they spend a lot of time, energy and money trying to hide.

I recently received an email from a reader in Tucson, Arizona complaining about the cases of pedophilia by Catholic priests in her area. This email came on the heels of a recent indictment of a Boston area Catholic priest who is suspected of molesting hundreds of altar boys over a thirty year period. It appears clear that this history of abuse was known by the Church hierarchy, including the present Cardinal and the one before him. Yet, in spite of numerous complaints by families of the victims, the offending priest was reassigned a number of times to new parishes, where the abuse of young boys continued. Families were encouraged to "keep silent" about the abuse in order to protect the Church that they loved. Many of them did so, until quite recently.

The sexual abuse of young boys by Catholic priests, along

with the secrecy surrounding it, is hardly a new issue. When I lived in New Mexico, there were numerous cases of pedophile priests recycled from parish to parish across the state. Many of these priests had completed a special "rehabilitation" program run by the Catholic Church and were considered no longer to be a threat to children. Yet they continued to rape the children of their parishioners.

This crime is serious one because it is committed by authority figures placed by their institutions in positions of trust. They are supposed to be shepherds of their flock, modeling unconditional love and compassion.

By virtue of their position, they commanded the respect, even the obedience, of their congregations. Yet these men have used their power and position to prey on minor children, often damaging them psychologically for life.

In some of these cases, the Church settles out of court and keeps the lid on the enormity of the problem. It continues to deny the sins of its shepherds, places new children at risk, and tears at the very fabric of trust that gave it the power it has.

Recently, however, the parents of the victims have become angry. They have refused to remain silent. They have refused to support the authority of a organization that has harbored criminals who have attacked their children.

Pedophiles hiding behind the cloth are simply wolves in sheep's clothing. But their behavior is not just their responsibility. The responsibility for their actions also lies with the institution that has harbored them.

By turning a blind eye to the pedophilia committed by its

offending priests and even reassigning some of these offenders to new parishes, Church leaders elevated the sins of a few priests to the level of corporate crime. Wittingly or unwittingly, the leadership of the Church aided and abetted its predatory priests in committing crimes against children.

Now as the scandal begins to reach truly epic proportions—with abuse victims coming forward in parishes all over the country—the Church can no longer hide its guilt or ignore its responsibility. It must come forward and make a full disclosure of all that it knows. Leaders who protected predatory priests must step down and allow new leadership committed to protecting children to step forward.

You would think that a church that preaches forgiveness of sin should be able to admit its own sins and face its guilt. However, the Catholic Church seems to be no more skilled at such endeavors than any other bureaucratic institution seeking to protect itself from potential lawsuits.

It is ironic that an institution that condemns homosexuality as a sin is a fertile breeding ground for the abuse of boys by its priests. It makes you wonder if the culture of celibacy might not be an incubator for aberrant sexuality.

Sooner or later, the Church will have to recognize that its requirement that priests be celibate is an inappropriate one. Celibacy just does not work for most people. And even if it worked for nine priests out of ten, that still leaves a lot of room for abuse.

Wouldn't the Church prefer to encourage its priests to engage in healthy sexual relationships with other consenting adults than to take the chance that they would rape the children who are given into their keeping? Wouldn't it prefer "out of the closet" homosexual behavior amongst priests to pedophilia?

And what about the many married Catholics, both men and women, who are capable of providing spiritual leadership—at the very highest level— should they be denied the right to serve their communities because of their gender or marital status? Doesn't the Church support marriage as an institution? And, if marriage is right for parishioners, then why not for priests?

An institution that excludes married people and women from its clergy has reduced its pool of potential priests by more than 75%. Add the requirement of celibacy to the list, and you are tapping well under 5% of the adult population. With such restrictions, you can be sure that some of the people who qualify aren't necessarily going to be the best role models. Among them you are bound to find a few pedophiles or people engaging in other types of deviant sexual behavior.

In order to change this shameful state of affairs, the Church will have to admit its sins and accept its guilt. It will need to apologize to the children who were raped and to their families. It will have to find ways to make amends and to learn from its mistakes so that it does not repeat them.

If the Church wants the forgiveness of its members, it must admit its guilt and come up with an atonement strategy that compensates its victims. It must make radical changes in the way it does chooses its priests, trains them, and oversees their behavior.

Anything less than that will not do. And that's not just because the courts will force the Church to reach deeply into its pockets. It is because those who support the Church will see the hypocrisy of the institution and stop supporting it.

In a free society, Justice is usually served in the end. Secrets are eventually told and leaders are forced to be accountable for their actions.

Sin, guilt and atonement play out not just in our personal life stories, but also in our collective ones. Corporations, governments, and religious institutions all make mistakes. They all try to deny those mistakes. And they are all forced, sooner or later, to confess their sins and to take responsibility for what they have done.

89

CORPORATE ACCOUNTABILITY

O rganizations reflect the moral character of their members, especially those members who are in leadership positions. If we want our organizations to act in a responsible manner, we must start holding the leaders of those organizations accountable for their actions. We must begin to ask CEOs, Non-Profit Directors and their Board members about the values of the organization and how those values are demonstrated. We must ask them "How do we know if what you do is consistent with what you say? Who oversees the bosses or the decision makers? What are the limits placed on power and privilege?" The same questions must be asked of religious and political leaders. Only when we hold such individuals accountable for their actions will they remain faithful to the values and standards they profess to uphold.

Neither capitalism nor democracy works without an informed and empowered constituency. Passive, uninformed consumers/citizens will inevitably be taken advantage of by authority figures—whether elected, hired or appointed— and the power structure that supports them.

It is hard to hold others responsible for their actions if you are not taking responsibility in your own life. If you cannot admit your mistakes and acknowledge your guilt, how can you expect your family, your friends, your coworkers, your church or your government to do so?

We do not have a right to expect others to be more responsible than we are. We would like to hold our leaders to a higher standard, but is this fair? We cannot help but feel compassion for public figures who lie or pass the buck when we see how hard it is for us to tell the truth and take responsibility for our actions.

Our charity and compassion help us refrain from the temptation to expect more from our leaders than we expect from ourselves. However, when we expect less from our leaders than we would expect from ourselves, our friends and our families, we put the safety of countless others in jeopardy.

The leaders of our companies, our community organizations and our government are in positions of trust. They are there not just to protect and uphold their own good, but the good of all the people whose lives are affected by their actions. When their actions are selfish, short sighted, or cowardly, they betray our trust and can no longer lead effectively.

This is not to say that we should expect anything close to perfection from those who have chosen to be our mentors and our leaders. We must realize that they will make mistakes just as we do. The question is not "Will they commit an error?" but "How honest and responsible are they when they make a mistake? Do they publicly acknowledge it? Do they show remorse and ask for understanding and forgiveness? Do they learn from their mistakes and take action to correct them? If so, we will not hold their mistakes against them. Indeed, we will be convinced that they are the right people to lead us, because they are capable of humility and self-examination.

When we ask people to take responsibility for their

actions, we are not condemning them. Quite the contrary. We are giving them the opportunity to acknowledge their mistakes and correct them.

Ironically, one of the reasons people do not admit their guilt is that they are afraid that they will be condemned or punished for their mistakes. As a result, they choose to deny their errors and hide their guilt.

If we really want honesty and disclosure, we need to create an environment in which people can be forgiven for their mistakes and simultaneously held accountable for them. Now we have neither forgiveness nor accountability. People deny their mistakes until someone discovers them. And then we are so outraged that we want to condemn them or punish them.

That does not create a culture of understanding and forgiveness. It also does not create a culture in which we strive to be our best and learn from our mistakes. When the threat of punishment or condemnation is the only method of accountability, no one wants to be held accountable. The culture of denial is thereby reinforced and maintained.

Of course, creating a culture in which compassion and accountability go together is an enormously challenging proposition. It means that we have to take on the powerful individual and collective assumption that we are bad if we make mistakes and that our errors require condemnation and punishment. A more charitable and accurate assumption would be: "We are not bad if we make mistakes, but we do have a responsibility to recognize our mistakes and learn from them. If we do, we will earn people's respect and trust."

REAL ATONEMENT

Genuine forgiveness of our trespasses is unlikely if there is not a full reckoning with what happened. That means that our secrets must be told and we, as individuals or organizations, must acknowledge our errors and accept our guilt. Moreover, forgiveness is unlikely unless and until we feel remorse and actively embrace a plan to atone for our errors. To attempt to forgive before these steps have been taken is to minimize the social and psychological challenges of real forgiveness and to raise expectations that are unlikely to be met.

Creating a culture of responsibility instead of denial and forgiveness instead of punishment is going to take a great deal of effort and commitment. It means changing the way we think and act about crime, the rehabilitation of criminals and the healing of victims.

We will have to ask more from all parties to insure that the whole story is told and full responsibility taken for what happened. Criminals will have to face their victims' pain and anger in ways that get through to them, instead of being separated from victims and protected from witnessing victims' feelings. It is essential that those who hurt others know the full extent and depth of the hurt they have caused. This is necessary not as a means of punishment, but as a means of acknowledging the complete story.

The truth telling commission adopted in South Africa after the Mandela government came to power provides a stunning example of how accountability and forgiveness can work simultaneously to help victims heal and perpetrators atone for their crimes. We have only begun to explore the therapeutic nature of such public tribunals that allow victims to confront their victimizers. By insuring that the full truth is told, these courts prevent any attempt on the apart of abusers or the institutions that support them to cover up, rationalize, or re-write the history of what happened. They also provide a mechanism by which restitution to victims can replace punishment as a primary method for righting wrongs that have been committed, particularly in situations of civil war or unrest, in which many crimes have been committed on both sides.

Any real atonement process requires a telling of the whole story from the viewpoint of the victim and his or her family. Moreover, there must be a therapeutic process that enables transgressors to fully experience the anger and pain of their victims and bring their repressed guilt into conscious awareness. When that happens, remorse and a desire to make amends and restitution happen as a natural result.

The rehabilitation process depends for its success on the authentic remorse of the transgressor. Without the recognition of the pain that has been caused and the desire to correct or restore, any attempt to rehabilitate will fall flat on its face. This is the sad truth.

Professional rehabilitators with their secular frames of reference are reticent to consider the spiritual dimension of the transformation they are seeking from transgressors. The shift from being irresponsible to being responsible, from denying truth to disclosing it, from dehumanizing victims to caring about them represents a major spiritual awakening. It probably does not happen without therapeutic interventions that enable the criminal to access and externalize his profound rage and grief in a way that is safe for him and others. After all, if he continues to block his awareness of his own pain, he is unlikely to understand or feel compassion for the pain of others.

It may be possible that a few people are "touched by the hand of God" and experience a sudden, profound conversion or psycho-emotional shift toward truth and responsibility. It does occasionally happen. However, we would be wise to be skeptical about such "conversions" and wait and see if the constructive behavior resulting from them is long lasting. These exceptions to the rule aside, most people will require a rigorous therapeutic process to penetrate the layers of denial that cover over their natural guilt.

Individual and group therapy can be used as tools that provide transgressors with a psycho-emotional environment in which a spiritual shift or epiphany can happen. Some therapists are skillful in using these tools; others are not. Moreover, even in the hands of skillful therapists, these tools do not work for all people. Some people are not going to make the shift we hope they will make, even though we create the most propitious environment for them. Yet, even if 25% of incarcerated inmates were successful in making this spiritual shift, it would transform the criminal justice system.

We don't even come to the issue of forgiveness until this shift has occurred. How can someone experience forgiveness for a crime he feels no remorse for committing? To experience forgiveness, you have to want it and know that it is necessary for your healing.

The same is true of other aspects of the atonement process such as making amends or restitution. If you don't want to help the victims of your crime, you deny yourself the healing affects of this atonement strategy. If you don't want to give to others, what joy, confidence and self worth will you derive from the effort? If your atonement strategy does not arise from your heart, but is simply mandated by the state, you will not perform it in good faith, nor will you derive spiritual benefit from it.

State mandated restitution is a form of punishment, not rehabilitation. For it to be real, an atonement strategy must be freely chosen. It must come from the heart of the one choosing it. Then it can be an act of healing for self and others.

Let us not kid ourselves here. The state cannot rehabilitate people. The state can create an environment in which fears can be faced and guilt can be made conscious. It can create a therapeutic atmosphere in which remorse can be felt and responsibility can be taken. It can prepare the criminal for his moral apotheosis, but it cannot give it to him. He must want it and open himself to it. And then he can use the tools that are provided in an effective way.

Rehabilitation is a spiritual process that begins in the heart of each person. Without a willing heart, it does not happen. But when the heart is willing, the tools of rehabilitation can be successfully used. The role of the state is to provide the very best therapeutic tools and to encourage their use.

Atonement strategies for transgressors should be developed in conjunction with case-workers/mentors who have had relevant, transformative life experience. The connection to these case-workers, along with networks of other like-minded mentors, must remain for years in order for rehabilitation to succeed. Sponsorship programs such as the one utilized in AA should be put in place so that long term emotional support is available to clients as needed.

Keeping a person in jail requires constant financial support. Keeping those who leave jail out of trouble will also involve continued financial support. The amount of this financial support probably can and will lessen over time. But the degree of emotional support required for successful rehabilitation should not be underestimated. It is much greater than anything offered now.

The parole system must be revamped to include weekly therapeutic support from mentors, as well as weekly group sessions for parolees. A close family-like environment must be maintained for atonement strategies to succeed and for the ex-criminal to be reintegrated in society as a contributing member.

The keyword here is support. Neither government agencies nor religious organizations can rehabilitate people. However, they can skillfully assist those people who are ready to take more responsibility for their lives.

REESTABLISHING SELF-ESTEEM & FAITH

The truth is that people who hurt others do not believe in themselves. Their actions are selfish but, ironically, selfish actions are a sign of lack of self confidence.

Most people who commit crimes have very low self esteem. They appear to compensate for that with lots of swagger and bravado, but this is just a show.

When you believe in yourself, you develop your talent and abilities and find ways to share them with others. You empower yourself, set goals, and move toward them. When you make mistakes, you don't blame them on other people, nor do you beat yourself mercilessly. You learn from your mistakes and move on.

When you believe in yourself, you don't have to try to "con" others. You don't have to make up a false identity. You don't have to strike out at other people in order to prove to yourself or your friends that you are strong or tough.

You don't have holes in your character that you are frantically trying to disguise with smoke and mirrors. You aren't afraid to be seen as you are. You know that you aren't perfect. But you are not ashamed of who you are. You can hold your head up high. You can stand up and be counted.

You can respect yourself and offer others the same respect. You can feel your equality with others. You don't feel inferior or superior.

People who hurt others have inferiority complexes which they attempt to disguise with airs of superiority. If you break their balloon, they will come after you, because they feel so insecure and vulnerable. If you criticize their persona, they feel that you have attacked their core. You don't want to offend them, even in little ways, because they can't take it. They can't hear even the tiniest criticism because underneath their masks they are so critical of themselves. One word from you sets them off. They may attack you, but only because they hate themselves.

Our prisons are filled with people with low self esteem. They act tough, but they are emotionally fragile. They are wounded kids who never got enough love and decided to do without it. Being tough becomes their identity, because they don't want to be seen as victims.

Of course, we know they are victims, because victims are the ones who victimize others. You don't try to create a victim unless you are one.

Teaching people like this how to love and honor themselves is no easy task, especially when they live together and feed off each other's powerlessness. How can they learn to believe in themselves without intensive therapy that helps them identify and release past patterns of victimization and appropriate role models that help them build real self-esteem?

Do we really think that people will make the spiritual transformation that leads to rehabilitation if they do not learn to love themselves? Do we really think they will be able to love and respect others if they are unable to love and respect themselves?

No matter how much we try to get away from it, we must recognize that moral transformation does not happen without spiritual experience. If no one loves you, you don't learn how to love.

In Communist China, powerful behavior modification techniques were used to rehabilitate criminals and bring them back into society. People left prison understanding clearly what would be expected of them and strong social pressures were used to keep them in line.

This is not psychological transformation, but social management. It does not ask the individual to change from within, but merely to conform to external expectations.

Real transformation means that one assumes a level of responsibility for one's behavior that one was not capable of assuming before. One takes this responsibility not because it is demanded by others, but because one's awakened self worth requires it. It is an inner transformation that bears external fruits.

The change here is not a temporary one. It does not immediately reverse when external factors change, because its source is not outside, but within. The inner self is empowered. It has the confidence that it can create meaning in its life.

So if we want real rehabilitation of behavior we need to commit to real transformation of consciousness. Love must be offered to those who feel unloved. Respect must be given to those who feel unworthy. Honesty, trust, and responsibility must be modeled by teachers and mentors.

Those who never knew love from a family must be offered a new spiritual family where love can be experienced. This is a process of re-parenting. Without the re-creation of the family structure—the true building block of society—real socialization based on love and the values that support it is impossible.

The most effective prison ministry programs are the ones that focus on offering love, not on teaching dogmatic ideas. They are the ones devoted to creating a culture of responsibility and forgiveness. When ministers offer words and actions that are empowering to prisoners and help them build their self-esteem, they create an environment in which people can connect with the Source of love inside themselves. It is that connection that initiates moral transformation and spiritual redemption. It cannot be offered as a religious dogma or course of study. But it can be discovered internally in an environment where prisoners feel accepted and loved by the people around them.

That is what spiritual community is all about. And spiritual communities in prisons are essential if they are going to be places of rehabilitation where people regain their faith in themselves, in their brothers and sisters, and in their God.

8

MAPPING THE TERRITORY

Without Contraries is no progression
WILLIAM BLAKE

What is Sin? Our understanding of the nature of sin, guilt and atonement leaves much to be desired. We think that we know what sin is but do we really? Do we understand that sin is something that happens every day of our lives? Do we realize that every time we trespass against someone else in our thoughts, our speech or our actions, a sin is committed?

To sin means to miss the mark. It means to make an error or a mistake. It means to go astray or off course. Committing a sin is not necessarily a bad thing. We make errors so that we can learn how to get closer to the mark or how to stay on course. It is an intricate part of the learning process. If we did not make mistakes, we would not learn or grow. We would not transform ourselves or our experience.

Sin occurs on all levels of our experience: physically, emotionally, mentally and spiritually. There are sinful actions, sinful feelings, sinful thoughts, and sinful belief systems.

Sins express in the outer world and the inner world. There are sins against other people and sins against ourselves.

There are sins in what we think, what we say, and what we do, to others and to ourselves.

There are sins of commission and sins of omission. We may think, speak or act in a way that is hurtful to others.

Or we may not think when something requires our awareness, not speak when we need to say something, and not act when something needs to be done.

For example, if we allow someone to be murdered or brutalized when we could have prevented the crime, our sin is one of inaction, rather than one of action. If we do not tell the truth when we have the opportunity to correct an error or misunderstanding, our sin is one of keeping silent. History is filled with horrible examples of times when people did not speak up or act to oppose injustice.

We commit sins not just by giving offense, but also by taking offense. We sin when we attack others and we also sin when we react violently to their attack against us. Indeed, that that is how the cycle of violence is perpetuated.

There are unintentional sins and intentional sins. Unintentional sins may involve:

- negative/judgmental thoughts about ourselves or others;

- careless/ impulsive speech such as bragging/boasting, gossiping or spreading rumors, criticizing ourselves or others, exaggerating or embellishing the truth, speaking in anger, blaming others without cause;

- careless/impulsive actions such as striking someone in anger or passive aggressive actions that express anger indirectly.

Intentional Sins may include:

- thoughts or beliefs that dehumanize people, including racist, sexist or terrorist concepts, engaging in any form of black magic, brainwashing or mind control.

- telling lies, libel, slander, rumor-mongering, character assassination, disseminating propaganda or disinformation, entering an agreement deceptively, withholding or obscuring information that could benefit others.

- cheating, stealing, raping or sexually abusing, murdering, imprisoning without cause, beating, torturing or brutalizing others, hurting oneself intentionally or committing suicide.

Indeed, the landscape of sin is as wide and far reaching as our experience itself. Indeed, sin and experience go hand in hand. Without one, you do not have the other.

WHAT IS GUILT?

Of course, the subject of guilt is as complex and wide-ranging as that of Sin. For every sin we commit, there is a unique and proportionate guilt that we will have to face sooner or later.

Basically guilt falls into two categories: natural guilt and false guilt. Natural guilt occurs when we see our mistake and the pain it has caused others, and we feel remorse for our actions. False guilt happens when we feel responsible for suffering we did not cause. Survivor's guilt is one example of false guilt. Other examples occur when people confess to crimes they did not commit, over-identifying with the victims or perpetrators of these crimes.

In order to heal, both types of guilt require awareness. Natural guilt requires the awareness that one has caused hurt to others and must take responsibility for one's actions. False guilt requires the awareness that one has not caused hurt to others but may have actually suffered the hurt one thinks one has caused.

Of course, life is often more chaotic and complicated than our descriptions of it. And it should be pointed out that some individuals can be feeling both natural and false guilt at the same time.

Nevertheless, guilt does not become hopelessly complex and convoluted until we deny or repress it. That's when the difficulty sets in.

Projection is one way that we try to deny our guilt. Instead of experiencing our guilt, we try to give it to someone else. All forms of blaming and shaming are ways of trying to make other people responsible for our own thoughts, feelings, and/or actions.

Another way that we attempt to deny our guilt is to try to justify our actions. We believe that we have a right to attack someone if we perceive that they have attacked us first. "I hurt you because you hurt me, or provoked me," we say. "You had it coming."

Our warped concept of justice is used to justify or condone our errors. It enables us to pretend not to feel guilty and to hide our guilt from ourselves and others.

In Dostoevsky's novel *Crime and Punishment,* the protagonist Roskolnikov intentionally murders a rich, old woman so that he can share her money with the poor. He thinks that this woman has no right to live because all she does is prey upon others. His justification for his crime is so strong that he is able to bury his guilt for a while. But his denial is only temporary. Throughout the novel, Roskolnikov's guilt becomes increasingly palpable until it rises up and swallows him. In the final analysis, his redemption—like ours—depends on his willingness to face his guilt and take responsibility for his actions.

Denying our guilt and denying our responsibility go hand in hand. If we don't admit our guilt, then we don't have to be responsible for what we have done or said.

And if we do not take responsibility we can trick ourselves into believing that "it is not our fault." We may have murdered someone, but "she deserved to die anyway."

Denial helps us to get away with murder, except for one simple thing. IT DOESN'T WORK! The best that it can do is cover over the truth for a while. We can disguise or repress our guilt, but we cannot make it go away. Sooner or later, it will surface.

Even if we seem to succeed in giving our guilt to someone else, it is only a matter of time before people see the guilt that lies behind the mask of innocence we wear. Until then, we will always be looking over our shoulder to see if someone is looking at us a little funny.

We may seem to get away with our crime, but in truth we are not free. We simply live in a prison no one else can see.

When we build our lives on a foundation of lies, the walls of our house are bound to come crashing down around us. All self-deception, like all deception of others, is at best temporary. The truth always reveals itself in time, because it is the only thing that stands up to scrutiny.

Denial promises "escape" from guilt, but it cannot deliver. In the end, we have to face the truth about ourselves.

WHAT IS ATONEMENT?

Atonement begins to happen when we tell the truth to ourselves and others and begin to take responsibility for what we have done. Instead of running away from our guilt, we face it head on.

We allow ourselves to feel our pain and our victims' pain. We apologize for our mistakes. We express our remorse. And we offer to make amends to those we have injured or hurt.

To atone means to correct our mistake, to make right what went wrong, to retrace our steps and come back on track. When we atone, we move from a state of psychological separation to a state of psychological connection.

Until we acknowledge our guilt, we feel separate from our true self and separate from others. When we tell the truth and embrace our guilt, we reconnect with our true self and with the people we have pushed away.

To atone is come back home, to experience a re-union, to be at-one with the whole from which we have temporarily separated. Until we atone, we do not complete our journey of learning and knowing. Atonement is the final stage of that journey. Without atonement, our sins and our guilt make no sense. They serve no purpose.

The heroic journey requires us to leave home. It requires us to make mistakes, to feel guilty, and to feel separate from each other. But it also asks us to learn from our mistakes, to forgive ourselves and others, and to come back into alignment. It requires not only that we learn to create, but that we learn to be responsible for our creations.

Once we learn to be responsible, we can come home. The journey of separation is no longer necessary.

HOW DO WE ATONE FOR OUR SINS?

There are a number of ways that we can experience our guilt and atone for our sins. Here are a few of them:

Admitting guilt and expressing remorse publicly

There are several types of public confessions that can be helpful to us.

- confessing to peers who have made similar mistakes and who love us and accept us (e.g. to members of our 12 step, Affinity, or other support group)

- confessing to clergy members or other trusted members of our church, temple or spiritual community

- expressing our remorse to victims and/or their families

- apologizing to the community we live in through the media or the court process

Making Amends/Restitution

Here are a few ways in which we can make amends to those we have injured.

- offering financial restitution to the victim and/or his or her family. While you cannot buy forgiveness, this atonement strategy can demonstrate a changed heart and increase the possibility for understanding and forgiveness.

- helping other victims of similar crimes. Sometimes the family of the victim may refuse to have any connection with you, but that doesn't have to stop you from making a commitment to help someone else in need. For example, a drunk driver who kills a child in an accident can sober up and become a big brother or volunteer at boy's club or an orphanage. There are all kinds of community service opportunities that can provide people with a vehicle for giving back to a community they have injured.

While courts may order community service, it means much more when it is undertaken voluntarily as an atonement strategy. Moreover, this strategy benefits the one making amends as much as it does the community, for the act of giving without expectation of return stimulates love, acceptance and belonging. It brings emotional and spiritual rewards to the giver that exceed any expectations s/he could have.

Crime tears the emotional fabric of families and communities. Selfless service helps to mend the fabric. Crime creates suspicion and mistrust. Atonement creates hope and trust.

Performing Penance

Penance is always voluntary. If someone requires us to do penance, it is punishment not penance. Penance is something that we elect to do. It is a choice that we make to set things right and establish balance back in our lives.

When we choose penance, we choose to deliberately humble ourselves to pay our debt to society. Instead of merely paying financial restitution for our crime, we might take a vow of poverty and spend the rest of our lives serving the poor. If we have been overly proud and disdainful, we might volunteer to clean the latrine at a homeless shelter. Penance is an extreme measure we take to learn humility and atone for the hurt we have caused others.

Working with Offenders

People who have committed crimes and faced their guilt squarely can become powerful role models for other offenders or potential offenders. By telling their story and sharing their experience, they can help others learn from their mistakes. They can also give others hope that there is a way out of the cycle of violence and abuse.

Practicing Forgiveness

Forgiveness allows us to put our trespasses behind us and to have closure. We can't move on with our lives and engage in positive actions until we stop blaming other people or beating ourselves up.

We are able to forgive because we have taken responsibility for what we have done. We have acknowledged our guilt, expressed our remorse, and taken steps to give back to those we have injured.

In other words, we have said and done all that we could say or do. The rest we will have to demonstrate by our actions in the future, showing those around us that we have learned from our mistakes.

Forgiveness is a choice to stop blaming, so that we can start loving. It means that we are willing to love and accept ourselves, even if it is the first time in our lives. And it means that we are willing to accept other people as they are and respect the choices that they make.

We can forgive without forgetting. Indeed, remembering what happened may help us stay in touch with the lesson of our experience. However, we don't dwell obsessively on what happened, wondering what we or others could have done differently.

If we do, then we haven't faced our anger or our guilt. And that means we need to take a few steps backward and understand that it is too early in our process to be trying to forgive. Forgiveness will come naturally if we do the hard work that comes before it.

When we forgive, we are saying that we are okay with ourselves. We are saying that we are okay with others. We are ready to move on from whatever pain or tragedy we have experienced.

Of course, this does not mean that our guilt or our anger never comes back. It does not mean that we don't have any residual guilt that we need to keep forgiving. It simply means that the balance has shifted from injury to healing, from victimization to empowerment. And each time our guilt arises, we more easily move away from blame toward acceptance and forgiveness.

Since we will continue to make mistakes, we need to understand that forgiveness must be an ongoing practice in our lives. We don't just forgive once and then go to heaven. We need to forgive each day.

9

OPENING
THE GARDEN GATE

At the end of all our exploring
will be to arrive where we started
and know the place for the first time.
T.S. ELLIOT

TWO TRINITIES

There are two trinities of consciousness that operate in our three dimensional world. One is the trinity of sin, guilt and atonement. This first trinity represents the act of taking responsibility for our experience. It declares "I am responsible for this mistake and I will learn from it."

Trinity of Responsibility

Atonement

FORGIVENESS

Sin   *Guilt*

The second trinity is the trinity of sin, denial, and projection/attack. It represents the inability to take responsibility and the attempt to make others responsible for our experience. It declares "I am not responsible for this mistake; you are."

Trinity of Projection

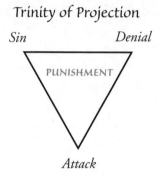

Sin   *Denial*

PUNISHMENT

Attack

The first triangle pictured on page 115 represents the correct use of knowledge and experience by human beings. It points upward because, by taking responsibility, humans connect with their divine purpose, establish heaven on earth, and ascend back to the divine realm.

The second triangle pictured above represents the incorrect use of knowledge and experience by human beings. It points downward because, by avoiding responsibility and seeking to blame others for their mistakes, humans prolong their incarnational experience and increase their suffering and that of others.

While the first triangle might be said to represent the establishment of heaven on earth, or in human consciousness, the second triangle might be said to represent the creation of hell on earth, or in human consciousness. One turns toward responsibility; the other turns away from it.

Both triangles start with the concept of sin, because the making of mistakes is the beginning of the quest for knowledge. It is an unavoidable part of human experience. It might indeed be said to characterize the human journey. You can't be a human being and not make mistakes. This first step into incarnational experience is a kind of fiat. It is a step into an imperfect world, a world where mistakes prevail and learning is the goal.

Of course, free will asserts itself upon our arrival here. We can choose to learn from our mistakes or not to learn. We can admit our guilt or project it. The choices that we make will determine the type of experience we will have here.

Until we make our first choice, the question of good or evil does not pertain. It is not an ontological issue. You are neither "good" nor "bad" because you make mistakes. Goodness has to do with learning and taking responsibility. Evil has to do with blaming others and refusing to learn or take responsibility.

Clearly, this is not a choice that we make once or twice in our lives. It is a choice that we make every day, indeed every moment, of our lives.

Not taking responsibility is a mistake. We all make it. We all turn away from responsibility at one point or another in our lives, and this turning away creates suffering in our lives. The pain of that suffering helps us recognize our mistake and learn to take responsibility next time.

We all have numerous opportunities to learn to be responsible for our thoughts, our words and our actions.

We can fail many times over and still succeed in the end.

Earth is, after all, a learning laboratory. The drama that we play out in relationship to each other is set up to help us learn. But it's still up to us. No one can force us to do something until we are ready.

Learning is very likely, because the pain of not learning can become unbearable. But the time that we take to learn is up to us. We can take a long time or a short time. People who learn quickly and become models of learning for others we consider "good." People who take forever to learn and hurt a lot of people along the way we consider "evil."

But no one is "good' from the start. Everyone begins by making a mistake. Everyone here hurts himself and someone else at least once, if not many thousands of times. And no one is "evil" in the end. In the end, no matter how much hurt you have given or received, you do not graduate from this classroom until you have learned to take responsibility for your actions.

When we look at the two interlocking triangles, we see our capacity for good as well as evil. We see that in every moment we are faced with taking responsibility or turning away from it, We are faced with creating heaven or creating hell, in our consciousness and our experience. In that sense, every moment of our journey presents us with an awesome choice.

We can be sure that we will be mistaken, but then what? Will we decide to admit our mistake or deny it? Will we take responsibility or blame someone else? Which trinity will we set in motion: the one that exacerbates our mistake or the one that corrects it?

THE FIRST CHOICE

Admission or Denial

So our initial choice is a critical one. Do we have the courage to admit that we have made an error? If so, we set in motion the trinity of responsibility that leads to redemption and forgiveness. If not, we set in motion the trinity of denial and blame that leads to punishment.

If our self-esteem is strong, we know that we can admit an error without being judged, rejected, or humiliated by others. If we have reasonable emotional maturity and confidence in ourselves, we know that we can probably correct our mistake and make things right again.

But, if our self-esteem is low, we may be afraid that others will reject us or punish us if we admit our mistake. We might be nervous about our error and unsure about whether or not we can fix it. So, instead of admitting our mistake, we might deny it or try to disguise it.

This is the defining moment, the moment in which we choose to move toward correction or toward punishment. If we are honest, we tell the truth and face the consequences. If we are not honest, we tell a lie and try to avoid the consequences.

Of course, if we choose to tell the truth, other people may express their anger toward us or push us away, but we will both be dealing with real feelings and whatever comes out of that will be real for both of us. But if we are not honest with others because we are afraid of their anger or rejection, we will be dealing with a fantasy or a pretense. It will have no substance. Even if we succeed in fooling others, they will find out the truth sooner or later. And when they do, they are more likely to reject us, because we deceived them.

It is ironic, but the attempt to run away from rejection and punishment eventually lead to it. We cannot escape the consequences of our actions, no matter how far we run away from them. In the end, we will have to face the consequences of what we have done.

Facing these consequences now is always easier and less hurtful to ourselves and others than facing them later. Repressed pain is more dangerous than expressed pain.

So we have a big choice to make. Will we be courageous and own our mistake or will we pretend that no mistake was made, or if one was made, it couldn't have been ours?

THE SECOND CHOICE
Taking Responsibility or Projecting it

If we admit our mistake, then we have work to do. We can apologize and offer to make things right. We can promise to be more careful, more patient or more sensitive next time. We can admit that we were selfish and did not realize how hurtful our action would be to others or to ourselves.

However, if our behavior is suspect and we don't admit our mistake, then we may try to make someone else responsible for the error. Denying the mistake probably won't satisfy us, because as long as the guilt is unassigned we will feel vulnerable. So we try to assign the guilt to someone else. We project the responsibility for what happened onto another person, believing mistakenly that this will create safety for us.

When others see that we are trying to blame them for our mistake, they understandably get upset. They may try to get even by blaming us for some other situation they are not ready to take responsibility for. Or they may try to convince us that someone else (a scapegoat) is responsible for our problem. Either way, a simple situation is made needlessly convoluted and complex. Blaming generally leads away from truth and toward increasing levels of denial and deception.

The insanity continues when we make emotional bargains and agree to carry each other's guilt. In fact, by doing so, our thoughts and actions become increasingly neurotic, creating an emotional maze from which neither of us can escape. In the end, we may hurt, maim or destroy each other because neither one of us has the courage to admit our mistakes and take responsibility for correcting them.

THE THIRD CHOICE

Punishment or Forgiveness.

Once we are engaged in the battle to prove who is responsible for the original error, neither one of us will be error free. Each of us will be looking for the ultimate proof that s/he is right and the other is wrong. At that point, it doesn't really matter who started the argument, because both sides are fully engaged in it. Both are right and both are wrong.

There can be no winner here. As long as mutual projection dominates, heavy casualties are taken on both sides. The only way out of conflict is to dissolve the projection and take responsibility for our actions.

No matter how out of hand things have gotten, we must return to where the conflict began. We must go back and acknowledge our mistake. This is the only action that will restore clarity.

When the first lie is withdrawn, all the lies that were told on top of it can come crashing down. Then can we move from a devastating battle that no one can win to the place of peace where no one loses.

War is a tragedy for everyone, but peace is a victory for both sides.

As long as we are not able to acknowledge our errors and the guilt we feel about them, we will be trying to make the guilt stick on the faces of our enemies. We will dehumanize them and brutalize them, trying to prove to ourselves and the rest of the world that they are guilty and we are innocent.

Whether the conflict is between individuals or between nations, this is a deadly charade. We are hard on those on whom we have projected our guilt, because deep in our hearts we know that it does not belong to them, but to us. Our insecurity requires desperate measures. Mercilessly, we exact from them the price we are unwilling to pay ourselves.

Yet, in the end, when accounts are settled, we will see that we took as many casualties as we caused. We tried to make them pay our dues, but we failed. We had to pay our dues anyway.

What we did to them was done to us. And the guilt we tried to give to them was given back to us. Limping and with bandaged arms and legs, we arrived back where we began. We came full circle.

We tried to give our responsibility away, but we couldn't do it. It simply was not possible.

Like it or not, the responsibility is ours and we have to take it. That is the way it is and the way it will always be.

IF I FORGIVE YOU I FORGIVE MYSELF

When all is said and done, what we learn from the battle is that our enemy is just a reflection of ourselves. We try to punish him, but it isn't possible. We cannot do something to him without doing the same thing to ourselves.

Forgiveness has the same circular path. We resist it, because we think that forgiving our enemy is being soft on him. But in reality, when we learn to forgive our enemy for what he did to us, we also learn to forgive ourselves for our own trespasses.

Our enemy always brings us face to face with ourselves. We cannot strike him without striking ourselves. We can't make peace with him without making peace with ourselves.

Jesus told us "do unto others as you would have them do unto you" because that is the spiritual law. Whatever we offer to another, we offer to ourselves, If we offer anger, we receive it. If we offer acceptance, we receive that.

He also told us to love our enemies. Why? Because hating our enemies keeps the inner battle raging. When we learn to love our enemies and forgive them, we offer the same love and forgiveness to ourselves.

And that is what we are here to learn to do: to make peace with our brothers and sisters and to make peace within our hearts. It is not as complicated as it seems to be. We make it complicated because we resist the simple truth.

As within, so without. What I see in myself I will find in you. And what I see in you is a reflection of what lies within my own mind and heart.

AS ABOVE, SO BELOW

It is an old esoteric truth that laws of earth reflect the laws of heaven. Natural law is not at odds with Spiritual law. It is a reflection of it. What is true of God must in some way be true of us, since we were created in God's image.

If we were created as male and female, then God must

also have male and female qualities and we are simply the expression of those qualities. If God has a unified, indivisible consciousness, then that unity consciousness must also be available to us.

If God can descend into the world of conditions, then we can ascend out of that world to place of our origin where there are no conditions. Indeed, if we are here, then we must also be there. And if God is there, S/He must also be here. In other words, we must be living in both worlds simultaneous. We are divine and human at the same time.

That means that at the very moment in which we make a mistake, we are not the mistake that we are making. To identify with the mistake is to prevent ourselves from being aware of it, learning from it and eventually being free of it. When we become aware of our mistake, we bring our divine consciousness to it and break our identification with it.

Once our awareness is present and we no longer identify with the mistake, we simply accept it. Then shame is impossible, because we are not the mistake, but the one witnessing the mistake and learning from it. Knowing that makes acknowledgement of our mistake easy. We know it is not a big deal. And we can see beyond it to the potential for greater understanding and effectiveness.

When we own our mistake, we take direct responsibility for our experience and don't project onto others. This saves us from getting involved in some horizontal drama in which we take our brother or sister as our enemy and go off into some foolhardy battle in which we forget who we are and why we are here.

We know that in all such journeys, someone carries the cross and someone is crucified. That is what Jesus showed us.

No, instead we stay focused on our own experience. We own our own judgments and take responsibility for our own mistakes. That keeps us centered and in direct vertical relationship with the divine truth.

Our horizontal experience then becomes one of honoring and respecting one another. We encourage each other to follow our hearts and realize our unique talents and abilities. We refuse to give our power to someone else or to take someone else's power from him or her. We don't want to control or be controlled.

That does not mean that we live in a mistake-free manner. Even when we learn to dance with the divine in ourselves and others, we still occasionally step on each other's toes. We don't stop being human just because we begin to realize our divinity. We acknowledge our humanity. We have our anger and our tears. We admit our mistakes. We apologize. We ask for forgiveness or we offer it.

Judgments still come up, but we know that we are not our judgments. We are aware of the judgment and we watch it. Because we see it without identifying with it, it cannot grab us. We don't give our power to it.

So we are divine and human at the same time. We see our judgments, but we know that we are not those judgments. We see our mistakes, but we know that we are not those mistakes. That means we can say to each other "I don't know why but I'm judging you and now I'm judging myself because I think I'm not being very spiritual." We can say what's happening without being ashamed of it, without needing to push it away.

That's what it means to be "in the world but not of the world." You are here and you see what's happening but you are not identified with what is going on. You see what you like and what you don't like, but you know that what you like or don't like isn't who you are.

You are a divine being having a human experience and you are a human being having a divine experience. It doesn't matter which way you say it, because each reflects the other. As above, so below. The human and the divine are not separate from each other.

That is what spirituality is, after all. It is the connection between the human and the divine and the divine and the human. Every great spiritual teacher who walked the earth came to demonstrate that connection.

Every one of us has that connection. But we are tempted to keep joining the horizontal drama of attack and defense, denial and projection. We keep going off like Don Quixote to fight imaginary windmills or rescue damsels in distress, only to come back to the same watering hole a little more tired and sore than we were before we left.

That's okay. We have all had our share of useless journeys. The good news is that we are back to where we started. Nothing is damaged beyond repair. We just need to acknowledge our mistake and ask for forgiveness.

God didn't leave when we went off hell-bent to convert the heathen and save the world from imminent destruction. S/He just hung around until we ran out of gas and decided to come back home. The key to the Garden was never taken away from us.

We just forgot that we had it. We had become so involved in our incarnational dramas that we couldn't remember the place where we had begun our journey. We knew there was a place called "home" but we did not know where it was or how to get there.

Now we know. The place is right here. And the time is now. The garden gate opens as soon as we put the key in the lock and turn it.

Sin takes us all on a circular journey. We move away from Truth so that we can know it more deeply. Every mistake we make helps us grow into greater awareness. The journey is difficult only when we are being hard on ourselves or on others. When we learn to ease up, it gets easier.

May you be easy with yourself. May you be easy with the people who share your life.

We all make mistakes. Let's not crucify each other any more over them. If you have to carry your cross, it's okay with me. But don't ask me to carry it for you or ask me to climb up on it. And, I promise, when it's time for me to carry mine, I will shoulder the load and hold you harmless.

What more can we do? When the crucifixions stop, the wailing will stop with them. And then the sound of the Shofar will be heard in the land.

I await that day with great eagerness, for that is the day when people of all races, languages, cultures and religions return to their place of origin. That is the place where we meet once again as equal human beings. That is the time when the body of Christ will be whole and the Buddha nature will emanate resplendently from every face.

God will rest within the human, and the human will rest in the Divine. We will regain the Garden of Eden in our hearts and minds and peace will return to the earth.

We will know at last that although we commit a mistake, we do not need to lose God's love or the love of our brothers and sisters. The world of denial and projection, attack and retribution will no longer exist, because we will cease creating it. By becoming responsible for our creations, we will not create the myriad hells of denial and projected guilt that seem to substantiate our fears and undermine our love.

Heaven will come to earth, not in the form of some divine retribution that punishes sinners and lifts the faithful up above them into some paradise on high. No. Heaven will come to earth because heaven is already on earth, here within us. As soon as we recognize its presence we become it, and then the inner light begins to shine forth so brightly that no one can deny it.

The culture of denial is created by fear and secrecy. It is destroyed by love and disclosure. Lies dissolve into truth. Darkness disappears into the light.

Men and women learn to stand up and become the expressions of God that they were created to be. Unafraid to create, make mistakes, apologize, and learn from their mistakes, they become responsible for their creations.

Instead of being a dumping ground for irresponsible actions, earth becomes an expression of our atonement. Instead of blindly carrying our collective wound, it opens to healing as we do. Crises come, as environmental sins are purged and balance is reestablished.

Slowly we awaken to what dominion means. It does not mean power over, license to waste or over-consume. It means enlightened stewardship. It means being responsible for what we make.

A stronger coming to our planet from some other solar system in another galaxy might be surprised to learn what human beings on planet earth have made while in the grip of fear: nuclear, chemical, biological weapons and waste, poisons buried in the earth and spread through the water and the air. Why? Because we fear our neighbor and want to protect ourselves from him.

"Strange form of protection!" our visitor might think. "Instead of building bridges of love and understanding, they have built walls that block out the light and deepen suspicion and mistrust. Surely, they will learn there is an easier way."

And surely we will learn. But as in all things, we cannot start with others. We must start with ourselves. We must ask ourselves: Who is the one who is willing to be responsible?' Everything else depends on our answer to this question.

When God spoke to the prophets he called their names. And they answered "Yes Lord. I am here. I am the one who decided to come here. I am the one who is responsible."

Today, God is calling our names. Your name, my name, all of our names. Today, God is calling all of us together. How will we answer? Will we say "Yes. Lord I am here. Or will we pretend that we cannot hear the voice calling to us? That is the question before each one of us.

Paul Ferrini's unique blend of radical Christianity and other wisdom traditions goes beyond self-help and recovery into the heart of healing. His conferences, retreats, and *Affinity Group Process* have helped thousands of people deepen their practice of forgiveness and open their hearts to the divine presence in themselves and others.

For more information on Paul's workshops, retreats, or *Affinity Group Process,* check out the web-site at *www.paulferrini.com.* You can send email to **heartway@crocker.com** or write to **Heartways Press, P. O. Box 99, Greenfield, MA 01302.**

New Releases from Heartways Press

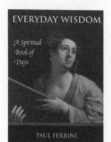

Everyday Wisdom
A Spiritual Book of Days
by Paul Ferrini
224 pages paperback $13.95
ISBN 1-879159-51-1

'Every Day Brings a Lesson!
Every day offers us incredible wisdom if only we can see the spiritual principles working behind the events and circumstances that are playing out in our lives. Seeing those principles requires a daily practice that helps us look beneath the surface of our lives and encourages us to face the truth, even when it is difficult.

Everyday Wisdom is a tool that can help you understand your spiritual lessons as they unfold each day of your life. Used in conjunction with journaling, it gives you a simple method of introspection, of looking within your own heart and mind, and finding the wisdom and the guidance that abide there. **This book can be used as a Spiritual Oracle** in conjunction with *Wisdom Cards,* the companion card deck.

Wisdom Cards: Spiritual Guidance
for Every Day of our Lives
ISBN 1-879159-50-3 $10.95
Each full color card features a beautiful painting evoking an archetypal theme.

Wisdom Cards will help you open to the source of wisdom within your own consciousness and determine propitious times for a significant event or project. These cards can be used alone (instruction booklet included) or in conjunction with the book *Everyday Wisdom.*

Christ is the light born in the darkness.
He is the rebirth of love in a world driven by fear.

The Living Christ: Conversations with a Teacher of Love
by Paul Ferrini
256 pages paperback $14.95
ISBN 1-879159-49-X

Paul: Is it true that you are the Christ?

Jesus: Yes, and so are you and everyone else who learns to love and accept self and others. If you practice what I came to teach, you will begin to realize that the Christ nature is the essence of each person. If you see it in me, you must also see it in yourself and in your brother or sister.

Paul: Are you saying the Christ is a sort of collective phenomenon?

Jesus: Yes, Christ is the light born in the darkness. It is the flame of self acceptance that extends to others and eventually to all.

Christ comes at the time of greatest darkness, the time when inner power is ignored and outer power dominates. He is rebirth of love in a world driven by fear.

Opening our Hearts to the Lessons of Love

Dancing with the Beloved
by Paul Ferrini
160 pages paperback $12.95
ISBN 1-879159-47-3

Romance may open the door to love, but it does not help us walk through it. Something else is needed. Something deeper. Something ultimately more real.

Challenging times must be weathered. Love must be strengthened beyond neediness and self-interest. It must die a thousand deaths to learn to rise like the phoenix beyond adversity of any kind.

Love is not a fragile, shiny thing, kept separate from the pain and misery of life. It is born of our willingness to learn from our mistakes and encounter the depth of our pain, as well as our partner's pain. That is the way it is.

In time we learn that all pain is the same pain. And we have compassion for the other people who inadvertently step on our toes as they learn to find the inner rhythms of the dance. Like us, they will stumble and fall hundreds of times until that moment of profound acceptance when grace comes and the beloved takes their hand in the circle.

Books and Tapes
available from Heartways Press

*Paul Ferrini's luminous new translation captures the
essence of Lao Tzu and the fundamental aspects of Taoism
in a way that no single book ever has!*

The Great Way of All Beings:
Renderings of Lao Tzu
by Paul Ferrini
320 pages hardcover $23.00
ISBN 1-879159-46-5

*The Great Way of All Beings: Renderings of Lao
Tzu* is composed of two different versions of
Lao Tzu's masterful scripture *Tao Te Ching*.
Part one, *River of Light,* is an intuitive, spon-
taneous rendering of the material that captures the spirit of the
Tao Te Ching, but does not presume to be a close translation. Part
Two is a more conservative translation of the *Tao Te Ching* that
attempts as much as possible to stay with the words and images
used in the original text. The words and images used in Part One
leap out from the center to explore how the wisdom of the Tao
touches us today. By contrast, the words and images of Part Two
turn inward toward the center, offering a more feminine, receptive version of the material.

*"We listen for it, yet its note can't be heard.
We look intently for it, yet its image can't be seen.*

*Although it has no beginning,
it leads us back to our original nature*

*Although it has no end,
it helps us come to completion."*

A Practical Guide to Realizing your True Nature

*"Enlightenment is the realization of the light that is within you.
It is the conscious recognition and acceptance of that light.
Enlightenment is discovering who you already are and being it fully."*

Enlightenment for Everyone
by Paul Ferrini
with an Introduction by Iyanla Vanzant
160 pages hardcover $16.00
ISBN 1-879159-45-7

Enlightenment is not contingent on finding the right teacher or having some kind of peak spiritual experience. There's nothing that you need to get, find or acquire to be enlightened. You don't need a priest or rabbi to intercede with God for you. You don't need a special technique or meditation practice. You don't need to memorize scripture or engage in esoteric breathing practices. You simply need to discover who you already are and be it fully. This essential guide to self-realization contains eighteen spiritual practices that will enable you to awaken to the truth of your being. This exquisite hard-cover book will be a life-long companion and will make an inspirational gift to friends and family.

A comprehensive selection from the Christ Mind teachings published by Doubleday

"*Open yourself now to the wisdom of Jesus, as Paul Ferrini has brought it through. These words can inspire you to greater insights and understandings, to more clarity and a grander resolve to make changes in your life that can truly change the world.*"

Neale Donald Walsch, author of *Conversations with God.*

Reflections of the Christ Mind:
The Present Day Teachings of
Jesus
by Paul Ferrini
Introduction by Neale Donald Walsch
302 pages hardcover $19.95
ISBN 0-385-49952-3

Reflections of the Christ Mind contains substantial excerpts from *Love Without Conditions, Silence of the Heart, Miracle of Love* and *Return to the Garden*. It presents the most important teachings in the *Christ Mind* series.

I am the Door
by Paul Ferrini
288 pages hardcover $21.95
ISBN 1-879159-41-4

Years ago, Paul Ferrini began hearing a persistent inner voice that said "I want you to acknowledge me." He also had a series of dreams in which Jesus appeared to teach him. Later, when Ferrini's relationship with his teacher was firmly established, the four books in the *Reflections of the Christ Mind* series were published. Here, in this lovely lyrical collection, we can hear the voice of Jesus speaking directly to us about practical topics of everyday life that are close to our hearts like work and livelihood, relationships, community, forgiveness, spiritual practices, and miracles. When you put this book down, there will no doubt in your mind that the teachings of the master are alive today. Your life will never be the same.

Taking Back Our Schools
by Paul Ferrini
128 pages paperback $10.95
ISBN 1-879159-43-0

This book is written for parents who are concerned about the education of their children. It presents a simple idea that could transform the school system in this country. This book does not pretend to have all the answers. It is the start of a conversation. It is chapter one in a larger book that has not yet been written. If you choose to work with these ideas,you may be one of the authors of the chapters to come.

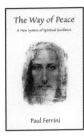

The Way of Peace
by Paul Ferrini
256 pages hardcover $19.95
ISBN 1-879159-42-2

The Way of Peace is a simple method for connecting with the wisdom and truth that lie within our hearts. The two hundred and sixteen oracular messages in this book were culled from the bestselling *Reflections of the Christ Mind* series by Paul Ferrini.

Open this little book spontaneously to receive inspirational guidance, or ask a formal question and follow the simple divinatory procedure described in the introduction. You will be amazed at the depth and the accuracy of the response you receive.

Like the *I-Ching,* the *Book of Runes,* and other systems of guidance, *The Way of Peace* empowers you to connect with peace within and act in harmony with your true self and the unique circumstances of your life.

Special dice, blessed by the author, are available for using *The Way of Peace* as an oracle. To order, send $3.00 plus shipping.

Grace Unfolding: The Art of Living A Surrendered Life
by Paul Ferrini
96 pages paperback $9.95
ISBN 1-879159-37-6

As we surrender to the truth of our being, we learn to relinquish the need to control our lives, figure things out, or predict the future. We begin to let go of our judgments and interpretations and accept life the way it is. When we can be fully present with whatever life brings, we are guided to take the next step on our journey. That is the way that grace unfolds in our lives.

"The Road to Nowhere is the path through your heart.
It is not a journey of escape. It is a journey through your pain
to end the pain of separation."

Illuminations on the
Road to Nowhere
by Paul Ferrini
160 pages paperback $12.95
ISBN 1-879159-44-9

There comes a time for all of us when the outer destinations no longer satisfy and we finally understand that the love and happiness we seek cannot be found outside of us. It must be found in our own hearts, on the other side of our pain.

This book makes it clear that we can no longer rely on outer teachers or teachings to find our spiritual identity. Nor can we find who we are in relationships where boundaries are blurred and one person makes decisions for another. If we want to be authentic, we can't allow anyone else to be an authority for us, nor can we allow ourselves to be an authority for others.

This provocative book challenges many of our basic assumptions about personal happiness and the meaning of our relationship with others and with God.

The Relationship Book You've Been Waiting For

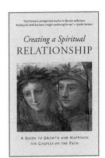

Creating a Spiritual Relationship: A Guide to Growth and Happiness for Couples on the Path
by Paul Ferrini
128 pages paperback $10.95
ISBN 1-879159-39-2

This simple but profound guide to growth and happiness for couples will help you and your partner:

- Make a realistic commitment to each other
- Develop a shared experience that nurtures your relationship
- Give each other the space to grow and express yourselves as individuals
- Communicate by listening without judgment and telling the truth in a non-blaming way
- Understand how you mirror each other
- Stop blaming your partner and take responsibility for your thoughts, feelings and actions
- Practice forgiveness together on an ongoing basis

These seven spiritual principles will help you weather the ups and downs of your relationship so that you and your partner can grow together and deepen the intimacy between you. The book also includes a special section on living alone and preparing to be in relationship and a section on separating with love when a relationship needs to change form or come to completion.

Return to the Garden
Reflections of The Christ Mind,
Part IV
by Paul Ferrini
200 pages paperback $12.95
ISBN 1-879159-35-X

"In the Garden, all our needs were provided for. We knew no struggle or hardship. We were God's beloved. But happiness was not enough for us. We wanted the freedom to live our own lives. To evolve, we had to learn to become love-givers, not just love-receivers.

We all know what happened then. We were cast out of the Garden and for the first time in our lives we felt shame, jealousy, anger, lack. We experienced highs and lows, joy and sorrow. Our lives became difficult. We had to work hard to survive. We had to make mistakes and learn from them.

Initially, we tried to blame others for our mistakes. But that did not make our lives any easier. It just deepened our pain and misery. We had to learn to face our fears, instead of projecting them onto each other.

Returning to the Garden, we are different than we were when we left hellbent on expressing our creativity at any cost. We return humble and sensitive to the needs of all. We return not just as created, but as co-creator, not just as son of man, but also as son of God."

Learn the Spiritual Practice
Associated with the Christ Mind Teachings

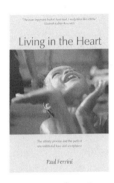

Living in the Heart The Affinity
Process and the Path of
Unconditional Love and Acceptance
by Paul Ferrini
128 pages paperback $10.95
ISBN 1-879159-36-8

The long awaited, definitive book on the *Affinity Process* is finally here. For years, the *Affinity Process* has been refined by participants so that it could be easily understood and experienced. Now, you can learn how to hold a safe, loving, non-judgmental space for yourself and others which will enable you to open your heart and move through your fears. The *Affinity Process* will help you learn to take responsibility for your fears and judgments so that you won't project them onto others. It will help you learn to listen deeply and without judgment to others. And it will teach you how to tell your truth clearly without blaming others for your experience.

Part One contains an in-depth description of the principles on which the *Affinity Process* is based. Part Two contains a detailed discussion of the *Affinity Group Guidelines.* And Part Three contains a manual for people who wish to facilitate an *Affinity Group* in their community.

If you are a serious student of the *Christ Mind* teachings, this book is essential for you. It will enable you to begin a spiritual practice which will transform your life and the lives of others. It will also offer you a way of extending the teachings of love and forgiveness throughout your community.

Now Finally our Bestselling Title on Audio Tape

Love Without Conditions,
Reflections of the Christ Mind, Part I
by Paul Ferrini
The Book on Tape Read by the Author
2 Cassettes, Approximately 3.25 hours
ISBN 1-879159-24-4 $19.95

Now on audio tape: the incredible book from Jesus calling us to awaken to our own Christhood. Listen to this gentle, profound book while driving in your car or before going to sleep at night. Elisabeth Kubler-Ross calls this "the most important book I have read. I study it like a Bible." Find out for yourself how this amazing book has helped thousands of people understand the radical teachings of Jesus and begin to integrate these teachings into their lives.

With its heartfelt combination of sensuality and spirituality, Paul Ferrini's poetry has been compared to the poetry of Rumi.

Crossing The Water: Poems About Healing and Forgiveness in Our Relationships
by Paul Ferrini
The time for healing and reconciliation has come, Ferrini writes. Our relationships help us heal childhood wounds, walk through our deepest fears, and cross over the water of our emotional pain. Just as the rocks in the river are pounded and caressed to rounded stone, the rough edges of our personalities are worn smooth in the context of a committed relationship. If we can keep our hearts open, we can heal together, experience genuine equality, and discover what it means to give and receive love without conditions.

With its heartfelt combination of sensuality and spirituality,

Paul Ferrini's poetry has been compared to the poetry of Rumi. These luminous poems demonstrate why Paul Ferrini is first a poet, a lover and a mystic. Come to this feast of the beloved with an open heart and open ears. 96 pp. paperback. ISBN 1-879159-25-2 $9.95.

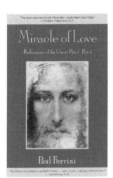

Miracle of Love: Reflections of the Christ Mind, Part III
by Paul Ferrini

In this volume of the Christ Mind series, Jesus sets the record straight regarding a number of events in his life. He tells us: "I was born to a simple woman in a barn. She was no more a virgin than your mother was." Moreover, the virgin birth was not the only myth surrounding his life and teaching. So were the concepts of vicarious atonement and physical resurrection.

Relentlessly, the master tears down the rigid dogma and hierarchical teachings that obscure his simple message of love and forgiveness. He encourages us to take him down from the pedestal and the cross and see him as an equal brother who found the way out of suffering by opening his heart totally. We too can open our hearts and find peace and happiness. "The power of love will make miracles in your life as wonderful as any attributed to me," he tells us. "Your birth into this embodiment is no less holy than mine. The love that you extend to others is no less important than the love I extend to you." 192 pp. paperback   ISBN 1-879159-23-6 $12.95.

The Ecstatic Moment: A Practical Manual for Opening Your Heart and Staying in It.
by Paul Ferrini

A simple, power-packed guide that helps us take appropriate responsibility for our experience and establish healthy boundaries with others. Part II contains many helpful exercises and meditations that teach us to stay centered, clear and open in heart and mind. The *Affinity Group Process* and other group practices help us learn important listening and communication skills that can transform our troubled relationships. Once you have read this book, you will keep it in your briefcase or on your bedside table, referring to it often. You will not find a more practical, down to earth guide to contemporary spirituality. You will want to order copies for all your friends. 128 pp. paperback ISBN 1-879159-18-X $10.95

The Silence of the Heart: Reflections of the Christ Mind, Part II
by Paul Ferrini

A powerful sequel to *Love Without Conditions*. John Bradshaw says: "with deep insight and sparkling clarity, this book demonstrates that the roots of all abuse are to be found in our own self-betrayal. Paul Ferrini leads us skillfully and courageously beyond shame, blame, and attachment to our wounds into the depths of self-forgiveness . . . a must read for all people who are ready to take responsibility for their own healing." 286 pp. paperback ISBN 1-879159-16-3 $14.95

Love Without Conditions: Reflections of the Christ Mind, Part I
by Paul Ferrini
An incredible book calling us to awaken to our Christhood. Rarely has any book conveyed the teachings of the master in such a simple but profound manner. This book will help you to bring your understanding from the head to the heart so that you can model the teachings of love and forgiveness in your daily life. 192 pp. paperback ISBN 1-879159-15-5 $12.00

The Wisdom of the Self
by Paul Ferrini
This ground-breaking book explores our authentic experience and our journey to wholeness. "Your life is your spiritual path. Don't be quick to abandon it for promises of bigger and better experiences. You are getting exactly the experiences you need to grow. If your growth seems too slow or uneventful for you, it is because you have not fully embraced the situations and relationships at hand . . . . To know the Self is to allow everything, to embrace the totality of who we are, all that we think and feel, all of our fear, all of our love." 229 pp. paperback ISBN 1-879159-14-7 $12.00

The Twelve Steps of Forgiveness
by Paul Ferrini
A practical manual for healing ourselves and our relationships. This book gives us a step-by-step process for moving through our fears, projections, judgments, and guilt so that we can take responsibility for creating the life we want. With great gentleness, we learn to embrace our lessons and to find equality with others. 128 pp. paperback ISBN 1-879159-10-4 $10.00

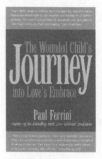

The Wounded Child's Journey: Into Love's Embrace
by Paul Ferrini

This book explores a healing process in which we confront our deep-seated guilt and fear, bringing love and forgiveness to the wounded child within. By surrendering our judgments of self and others, we overcome feelings of separation and dismantle co-dependent patterns that restrict our self-expression and ability to give and receive love. 225 pp. paperback ISBN 1-879159-06-6 $12.00

The Bridge to Reality
by Paul Ferrini

A Heart-Centered Approach to *A Course in Miracles* and the Process of Inner Healing. Sharing his experiences of spiritual awakening, Paul emphasizes self-acceptance and forgiveness as cornerstones of spiritual practice. Presented with beautiful photos, this book conveys the essence of *The Course* as it is lived in daily life. 192 pp. paperback ISBN 1-879159-03-1 $12.00

Virtues of The Way
by Paul Ferrini

A lyrical work of contemporary scripture reminiscent of the *Tao Te Ching*. Beautifully illustrated, this inspirational book will help you cultivate the spiritual values required to fulfill your creative purpose and live in harmony with others. 64 pp. paperback ISBN 1-879159-04-X $7.50

From Ego to Self
by Paul Ferrini

108 illustrated affirmations designed to offer you a new way of viewing conflict situations so that you can overcome negative thinking and bring more energy, faith and optimism into your life. 144 pp. paperback ISBN 1-879159-01-5 $10.00

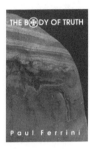

The Body of Truth
by Paul Ferrini

A crystal clear introduction to the universal teachings of love and forgiveness. This book traces all forms of suffering to negative attitudes and false beliefs, which we have the ability to transform. 64 pp. paperback ISBN 1-879159-02-3 $7.50

Available Light
by Paul Ferrini

Inspirational, passionate poems dealing with the work of inner integration, love and relationships, death and re-birth, loss and abundance, life purpose and the reality of spiritual vision. 128 pp. paperback ISBN 1-879159-05-8 $10.00

Poetry and Guided Meditation Tapes
by Paul Ferrini

The Poetry of the Soul

With its heartfelt combination of sensuality and spirituality, Paul Ferrini's poetry has been compared to the poetry of Rumi. These luminous poems read by the author demonstrate why Paul Ferrini is first a poet, a lover and a mystic. Come to this feast of the beloved with an open heart and open ears. With Suzi Kesler on piano. ISBN 1-879159-26-0 $10.00

The Circle of Healing

The meditation and healing tape that many of you have been seeking. This gentle meditation opens the heart to love's presence and extends that love to all the beings in your experience. A powerful tape with inspirational piano accompaniment by Michael Gray. ISBN 1-879159-08-2 $10.00

Healing the Wounded Child

A potent healing tape that accesses old feelings of pain, fragmentation, self-judgment and separation and brings them into the light of conscious awareness and acceptance. Side two includes a hauntingly beautiful "inner child" reading from The Bridge to Reality with piano accompaniment by Michael Gray. ISBN 1-879159-11-2 $10.00

Forgiveness: Returning to the Original Blessing

A self healing tape that helps us accept and learn from the mistakes we have made in the past. By letting go of our judgments and ending our ego-based search for perfection, we can bring our darkness to the light, dissolving anger, guilt, and shame. Piano accompaniment by Michael Gray. ISBN 1-879159-12-0 $10.00

Paul Ferrini Talks and Workshop Tapes

Answering Our Own Call for Love

Paul tells the story of his own spiritual awakening: his Atheist upbringing, how he began to open to the presence of God, and his connection with Jesus and the Christ Mind teaching. In a very clear, heart-felt way, Paul presents to us the spiritual path of love, acceptance, and forgiveness. 1 Cassette ISBN 1-879159-33-4 $10.00

The Ecstatic Moment

Shows us how we can be with our pain compassionately and learn to nurture the light within ourselves, even when it appears that we are walking through darkness. Discusses subjects such as living in the present, acceptance, not fixing self or others, being with our discomfort and learning that we are lovable as we are. 1 Cassette ISBN 1-879159-27-3 $10.00

Honoring Self and Other

Helps us understand the importance of not betraying ourselves in our relationships with others. Focuses on understanding healthy boundaries, setting limits, and saying no to others in a loving way. Real life examples include a woman who is married to a man who is chronically critical of her, and a gay man who wants to tell his judgmental parents that he has AIDS. 1 Cassette ISBN 1-879159-34-1 $10.00

Seek First the Kingdom

Discusses the words of Jesus in the Sermon on the Mount: "Seek first the kingdom and all else will be added to you." Helps us understand how we create the inner temple by learning to hold our judgments of self and other more compassionately. The love of God flows through our love and acceptance of ourselves. As we establish our connection to the divine within ourselves, we don't need to look outside of ourselves for love and acceptance. Includes fabulous music by The Agape Choir and Band. 1 Cassette ISBN 1-879159-30-3 $10.00

Double Cassette Tape Sets

Ending the Betrayal of the Self

A roadmap for integrating the opposing voices in our psyche so that we can experience our own wholeness. Delineates what our responsibility is and isn't in our relationships with others, and helps us learn to set clear, firm, but loving boundaries. Our relationships can become areas of sharing and fulfillment, rather than mutual invitations to co-dependency and self betrayal. 2 Cassettes   ISBN 1-879159-28-7 $16.95

Relationships: Changing Past Patterns

Begins with a Christ Mind talk describing the link between learning to love and accept ourselves and learning to love and accept others. Helps us understand how we are invested in the past and continue to replay our old relationship stories. Helps us get clear on what we want and understand how to be faithful to it. By being totally committed to ourselves, we give birth to the beloved within and also without. Includes an in-depth discussion about meditation, awareness, hearing our inner voice, and the Affinity Group Process. 2 Cassettes
ISBN 1-879159-32-5 $16.95

Relationship As a Spiritual Path

Explores concrete ways in which we can develop a relationship with ourselves and learn to take responsibility for our own experience, instead of blaming others for our perceived unworthiness. Also discussed: accepting our differences, the new paradigm of relationship, the myth of the perfect partner, telling our truth, compassion vs. rescuing, the unavailable partner, abandonment issues, negotiating needs, when to say no, when to stay and work on a relationship and when to leave. 2 Cassettes
ISBN 1-879159-29-5 $16.95

Opening to Christ Consciousness

Begins with a Christ Mind talk giving us a clear picture of how the divine spark dwells within each of us and how we can open up to God-consciousness on a regular basis. Deals with letting go and forgiveness in our relationships with our parents, our children and our partners. A joyful, funny, and scintillating tape you will want to listen to many times. 2 Cassettes
ISBN 1-879159-31-7 $16.9

Poster and Notecards

Risen Christ Posters & Notecards
11" x 17"
Poster suitable for framing
ISBN 1-879159-19-8 $10.00

Set of 8
Notecards with Envelopes
ISBN 1-879159-20-1
$10.00

Ecstatic Moment Posters & Notecards
8.5" x 11"
Poster suitable for framing
ISBN 1-879159-21-X $5.00

Set of 8
Notecards with Envelopes
ISBN 1-879159-22-8
$10.00

Heartways Press Order Form

Name _____

Address _____

City _____ State _____ Zip _____

Phone/Fax_____ Email _____

Books by Paul Ferrini

Everyday Wisdom ($13.95)   _____

Wisdom Cards ($10.95)   _____

Forbidden Fruit ($12.95)   _____

The Living Christ ($14.95)   _____

Dancing with the Beloved ($12.95)   _____

The Great Way of All Beings: Hardcover ($23.00)   _____

Enlightenment for Everyone Hardcover ($16.00)   _____

Taking Back Our Schools ($10.95)   _____

The Way of Peace Hardcover ($19.95)   _____

   Way of Peace Dice ($3.00)   _____

Illuminations on the Road to Nowhere ($12.95)   _____

I am the Door Hardcover ($21.95)   _____

Reflections of the Christ Mind Hardcover ($19.95)   _____

Creating a Spiritual Relationship ($10.95)   _____

Grace Unfolding: Living a Surrendered Life ($9.95)   _____

Return to the Garden ($12.95)   _____

Living in the Heart ($10.95)   _____

Miracle of Love ($12.95)   _____

Crossing the Water ($9.95)   _____

The Ecstatic Moment ($10.95)   _____

The Silence of the Heart ($14.95)   _____

Love Without Conditions ($12.00)   _____

The Wisdom of the Self ($12.00)   _____

The Twelve Steps of Forgiveness ($10.00)   _____

The Circle of Atonement ($12.00)   _____

The Bridge to Reality ($12.00)   _____

From Ego to Self ($10.00)   _____

Virtues of the Way ($7.50)   _____

The Body of Truth ($7.50)   _____

Available Light ($10.00)   _____

Audio Tapes by Paul Ferrini

The Circle of Healing ($10.00)   _____

Healing the Wounded Child ($10.00)   _____

Forgiveness: The Original Blessing ($10.00)   _____

The Poetry of the Soul ($10.00)   _____

Seek First the Kingdom ($10.00)   _____

Answering Our Own Call for Love ($10.00)   _____

The Ecstatic Moment ($10.00)   _____

Honoring Self and Other ($10.00)   _____

Love Without Conditions ($19.95) 2 tapes   _____

Ending the Betrayal of the Self ($16.95) 2 tapes   _____

Relationships: Changing Past Patterns ($16.95) 2 tapes   _____

Relationship As a Spiritual Path ($16.95) 2 tapes   _____

Opening to Christ Consciousness ($16.95) 2 tapes   _____

Posters and Notecards

Risen Christ Poster 11"x17" ($10.00)   _____

Ecstatic Moment Poster 8.5"x11" ($5.00)   _____

Risen Christ Notecards 8/pkg ($10.00)   _____

Ecstatic Moment Notecards 8/pkg ($10.00)   _____

Shipping

Priority Mail shipping for up to two items $3.95.   _____

Add $1.00 for each additional item   _____

Massachusetts residents please add 5% sales tax.   _____

Add an extra $2.00 for shipping to Canada/Mexico   _____

Add an extra $4.00 for shipping to Europe   _____

Add an extra $6.00 for shipping to other countries   _____

TOTAL   _____

Send Order To: Heartways Press P. O. Box 99,
Greenfield, MA 01302-0099   413-774-9474
Toll free: 1-888-HARTWAY (Orders only)
www.paulferrini.com
www.heartwayspress.com
email: heartway@crocker.com